DISCIPLE MAKING

TRAINING LEADERS TO MAKE DISCIPLES

▶ A Self-study Course in Understanding and Applying Jesus' Command to "Make Disciples"

DEVELOPED BY THE INSTITUTE OF EVANGELISM BILLY GRAHAM CENTER

ROBERT E. COLEMAN
TIMOTHY K. BEOUGHER
TOM PHILLIPS
WILLIAM A. SHELL,
EDITORS

Disciplemaking: Training Leaders to Make Disciples
Copyright © 1994 by the Billy Graham Center, Institute of Evangelism,
Wheaton, IL.

This course manual accompanies cassette tapes which contain instruction
and examples of disciplemaking and follow-up. The views expressed on the
tapes do not necessarily reflect the official positions of the Billy Graham
Center, Institute of Evangelism.

Unless otherwise noted, Scripture quotations are taken from the Holy Bible,
New International Version © 1973, 1978, 1984 International Bible Society.
Used by permission of Zondervan Bible Publishers.

The artwork in this manual was done by Bob Fuller Creative and is the sole
property of the Billy Graham Center, Institute of Evangelism.

ISBN 1-879089-13-0
Printed in the United States of America

$\mathscr{T}$able of $\mathscr{C}$ontents

ACKNOWLEDGMENTS

As with many educational projects, this has been a team effort. Dr. Robert Coleman, Director of the School of World Mission and Evangelism at Trinity Evangelical Divinity School and Director of the Billy Graham Center's Institute of Evangelism, conceived the original course outline and content, and supervised its progress. Dr. William Shell, Associate Professor of Bible at Reformed Bible College, developed the first draft of the material and gave many helpful suggestions along the way. Dr. Timothy Beougher, Assistant Professor of Evangelism at Wheaton Graduate School and Associate Director of Educational Programs for the Institute of Evangelism oversaw the editing process to bring the project to its final form. Dr. Tom Phillips, Director of Counselling and Follow-up for the Billy Graham Evangelistic Association, gave valuable input into the course structure in the early stages and worked over the final draft. Mr. Gene Warr, a businessman and veteran disciplemaker, provided many helpful suggestions during the process of the course development. Dr. James Kraakevik, Director of the Billy Graham Center, provided administrative support throughout the project, as did LTC(Ret) David Olmsted, Associate Director of Administration in the Institute of Evangelism. Dr. Merrill Ewert, Professor of Education at Cornell University, provided assistance in instructional design. Mr. Mark Cedar, Field Coordinator for the Institute of Evangelism, prepared many technical aspects, particularly the audio component and course manual design. Mr. Dale Haas, Broadcast Services Coordinator for Wheaton College, provided the technical mixing and editing for the master tapes of the audio component. Mrs. Diane Garvin, secretary for the Institute of Evangelism, gave countless hours of her time to this project, helping in innumerable ways. Dr. Melvin Lorentzen, Associate Director of the Billy Graham Center and long-time professor of English at Wheaton College, contributed valuable input in the editing process.

After several drafts, selected representatives from various segments of society and the church field tested the material. We acknowledge with thanks those who graciously devoted their time evaluating the material and providing valuable feedback.

We are also deeply appreciative of the speakers who graciously allowed us to use their messages in this course. The six audio tapes accompanying this manual include excerpts from a wide variety of messages given over the last few decades, all of which are used by permission. A special thanks to Moody Bible Institute and the Billy Graham School of Evangelism for their assistance in providing some of the excerpts. With the exception of the Dawson Trotman segments, all are of excellent audio quality. To insure the understanding of the Trotman excerpts, a transcription of his remarks is at Appendix E.

Alexander, Eric	*Abide in Me*
Barnett, Max	*How Discipleship Works in the Church* *Set a Goal, Set the Pace, Share Your Life* *The Church and the New Convert* *The Process of Making Disciples #2 & #3*
Beougher, Tim	*Praying for Crop Failure*
Bell, Ralph	*What It Means to be...*
Berg, Ron	*Making Disciples*
Bright, Bill	*Filling of the Holy Spirit* *Walking in the Spirit*
Briscoe, Stuart	*Being a Disciple*
Cedar, Paul	*It's Time to Die*
Cloud, Steve	*How to Develop a Vision for Your Ministry*
Coleman, Lyman	*Small Group Leadership Seminar—2/01/92*
Coleman, Robert	*Discipling Through Cell Groups* *The Authority of Christ*
Corts, John	*Scripture Memory Motivator*
Crawford, John	*How to Do Biblical Follow-Up*
Cunningham, Milton	*Nurturing New Christians*
Dawson, Dave	*The Layman and the Great Commission #1–#3*
Eims, LeRoy	*Principles of Disciplemaking #1–#4* *Your World and Its Needs*

Evans, Tony	*Enablement for Spiritual Growth* *Making Disciples*
Glockner, Robert	*Ways to Begin a Personal Journey in Discipleship and Discipling*
Gorsuch, Diane	*Disciplemaking for Women*
Graham, Billy	*Giving the Invitation—Amsterdam '86* *Results of Evangelism*
Gray, Philip "Skip"	*Designed for Discipleship*
Griffin, Jack	*The Vision of Disciplemaking*
Halverson, Richard	*Who Can Be Saved?*
Hanks, Billie	*The Importance of Vision*
Hendricks, Howard	*Discipleship #1—#3 & #5* *The Power of Groups* *Worship Served Family Style*
Henrichsen, Walt	*Nuts and Bolts of Discipleship* *Principles of the Walk with God* *Vision*
Hoo, Ray	*Being Servants*
Hull, Bill	*Discipling the Church #1*
Lord, Peter	*Characteristics of Developing Character*
Lutzer, Erwin	*God's Spirit: Filled or Empty?*
Mayhall, Jack	*The Direction of a Disciple*
Meredith, Dollee	*The Christian Woman in Today's Society*
Moore, Waylon	*Theory of Follow-Up*
Neighbor, Ralph Jr.	*Sharing Principles for Discipling and Equipping the Church #2*
Ockenga, Harold	*Holy Spirit in the Life of the Believer*
Olford, Stephen	*A Spirit-Filled Walk* *Quiet Time*
Phillips, Tom	*Strategies for Discipling* *Tools for Follow-Up and Discipling*

Price, E.W. "Buddy"	*How to Develop Your Character*
Riggs, Charlie	*Basic Steps in Christian Living* *Helping a New Christian Grow* *Learning to Walk with God: Power for Multiplying*
Robinson, Haddon	*Prayer*
Sanny, Lorne	*A Little One Shall Become a Thousand* *Man-to-Man* *Multiply the Laborers* *Training Spiritual Qualified Laymen #3*
Sapp, Jon	*How to Help Others Grow*
Streeter, Judy	*How to Nourish Growth in Others*
Trotman, Dawson	*Born to Reproduce* *Witnessing and Multiplication*
Trueblood, Elton	*Holy Call of the Layman*
Vidano, Bob	*God's Plan to Reach the World*
Warr, Gene	*Priorities and the Use of Time* *Teachableness* *Wheel and Hand Illustrations*

What you have in your hands now results from the combined labor of all those persons—pastors, evangelists, missionaries, seminarians, laypersons and educators. We believe the course constructively confronts the key issues in follow-up and disciplemaking. By God's grace, we offer it to help you be more effective in your high calling to "go and make disciples."

INTRODUCTION TO THE COURSE

"All authority in heaven and on earth has been
given to me. Therefore go and make disciples of
all nations, baptizing them in the name of the
Father and of the Son and of the Holy Spirit, and
teaching them to obey everything I have commanded you. And surely I am with you always,
to the very end of the age" (Matt. 28:18–20).

Our Lord's Great Commission has not changed since the day he
committed this task to his early followers. We as believers today are
to follow a Great Commission Lifestyle, making disciples "as we go"
through life.

What we learn in our walk with God we are to reproduce in the
lives of others. So it is our responsibility as more mature believers
to follow-up new Christians and to disciple them till they become
able themselves to reproduce spiritually (see 2 Timothy 2:2). Thus
the process is...

♦ **Evangelizing**...the lost.

♦ **Establishing**...new Christians ("Follow-up").

♦ **Equipping**...growing Christians for ministry
    ("Disciplemaking").

The purpose of the course is to help church leaders better
understand and apply Jesus' command to make disciples. As such
it is a training program for persons responsible for reproducing the
Christian life — persons who have advanced beyond the first steps
of following Christ and want to learn how to train others to fulfill the
Great Commission.

The course begins by showing *why* this work is crucial, laying
the foundation for a biblical philosophy of ministry. The study then
moves to practical considerations in actually doing the work,
explaining *how* to proceed, first to practical ways for establishing
new believers in their Christian life, then to the more advanced
stage of equipping disciples for spiritual reproduction. Finally, the
last section relates everything to the church's on-going program.

For you to make the most of this course and grow in your skills
as a disciplemaker, here are four key steps.

I. STUDY IN GOOD WAYS

The course has four Units of three Sessions each. If you try to study too many lessons at once, you might become confused with too much material. If you wait too long between sessions, you might forget some important points or lose the flow of the process. Work through the material at a pace that fits your schedule.

> Your hopes should be high as you begin this course — purpose to be used of God to affect your world for his glory. Now is the time to begin enjoying personal and professional fulfillment as you study, grow, and reproduce what you have learned.

♦ *Make time for study*

It will be best for you to study one lesson weekly over the next three months. Try to set aside two or more hours for a session each week on a regular schedule as if you were going to a class. That should give you time to read carefully, listen to the tapes, do all the exercises, and work on the assignments.

♦ *Write lesson exercises*

Since you are studying this course by yourself instead of in a class with other people, you need to pause often to review what you have read. If possible, complete each exercise from memory, writing your responses in the Manual. Of course, you may check the text to make sure your answers are correct. You will not receive a "grade" for this work, so you need to be your own monitor to make sure you are learning the necessary points.

These periodic exercises are built-in units of review as you proceed through each lesson. They are closely tied to the application sections at the end of each session and to the review material in Session 13.

♦ *Listen to tapes*

Audio cassette tapes which supplement the Manual come with the course. The tape segments illustrate lesson principles of disciplemaking. You will need to have a tape player available at each study period, along with a note pad and pencil. Let these messages inspire you as well as instruct you!

> The excerpts on the tapes come from messages by leading practitioners in the ministry of follow-up and discipling. They include pastors, leaders of Christian organizations and lay persons who have been active in this ministry of helping new Christians grow and become spiritual reproducers.

◆ Use the Scriptures

Always have your Bible beside you as you study this Manual. Most scriptural references here are from the New International Version (NIV). You might want to use more than one translation to compare other readings. The Christian always should check what he or she is learning with the teaching of the Holy Scriptures, following the example of the "noble Bereans."

> "Now these [the people in Berea] were more noble-minded than those in Thessalonica, for they received the word with great eagerness, examining the Scriptures daily, to see whether these things were so" (Acts 17:11).

II. FIND A MENTOR

Complete the Student and Mentor Agreement form at the back of this Manual, tear it out, and mail it *immediately* to the Institute of Evangelism, Billy Graham Center, Wheaton, Illinois, 60187, USA. Be sure to do this *before* you begin your study. This will officially register you for this course to receive future certification for your work.

Although designed primarily for self-study, this course may be used in a classroom or group study format. When used in such a mannner, your class leader should complete the Student and Mentor Agreement, and the Mentor Final Review.

Here is what your Mentor will be expected to do.

◆ Counsel

Before you start your first session, you and your Mentor should talk together about your experience in follow-up and disciplemaking. What experience have you had thus far? What opportunities lie ahead of you? What needs for personal growth do you have in mind? How do you think this course will help you? You will be more focused if you get the Mentor's reflections on such questions.

♦ Review

At the end of each Unit, [approximately every three weeks if you do one session each week] the Mentor will meet with you again for about an hour. At that time, the two of you will discuss what you have been reading in the lessons and hearing on the tapes. You will share any questions that have come to your mind about the material, and any ideas that your study has generated.

Most of the time, though, will be for the Mentor to review your progress on the exercises given for each session. This conversation should give you someone else's honest opinion about how well you are applying the principles you are studying.

Your Mentor's counsel for these three review sessions will encourage you to keep moving ahead on schedule, and to do your best possible work.

♦ Report

When the course is completed, the Mentor will fill out with appropriate comments a Review Form provided in this Manual.

You can see that the Mentor you select will have to invest time and thought in helping you. Make sure, therefore, that the person is a growing Christian brother or sister who shares your desire to see lost persons won to Christ and discipled.

III. EMPHASIS ON SPIRITUAL REPRODUCTION

If this course asked you only to read the Manual, listen to the tapes, write out the exercises, and talk with your Mentor, you would never know whether or not it helped you become a more effective disciple-maker. Ultimately the only way we learn to disciple others is by doing it!

With that in mind, you will note that at the end of Session 3 you must begin to follow-up a new or immature believer. Begin praying right now that God will make it clear to you who this person should be. It could be someone you have recently led to faith in Christ or someone in your church. The Manual will give you insight on what to do with this person when you meet together.

At the end of Session 9, you will challenge this person to begin to reach out to a new or immature Christian that he or she knows, to continue the process of multiplication. You will then be reproducing your discipling in a second generation.

IV. EARN YOUR CREDIT

Recognition for work well done can take many forms. Seeing another believer grow in the Lord because of your influence will be a reward greater than anything else you could ask.

When you have completed all the work in this course, and have worked at establishing a new or immature believer in the faith, we estimate that you will have invested at least forty hours of your time. That stewardship of yours deserves to be officially recorded. There are two ways the Billy Graham Center will do that:

◆ *Continuing Education Units (CEU)*

For forty hours of work in this course, you will receive four (4) Continuing Education Units. This is NOT academic credit to apply toward studies in a college or seminary. This is professional credit which shows that you are improving your knowledge and skills for serving the Lord.

◆ *Certificate of Achievement*

So that you may have your own record of those credits, and to verify your work for church leaders and ministry colleagues who might be interested, you will receive a properly inscribed certificate bearing your name, with the course title, ***Disciplemaking***, notation of the CEU number (4), and the validating signatures of Institute of Evangelism administrators. This will be sent to you when the Center receives the Mentor Final Review Form.

Your diligence in fulfilling all the requirements of this course is a matter of your personal honor as a Christian, and of the integrity of your Mentor who will endorse your claim for credit.you do one session each week] the Mentor will meet with you again for about an hour. At that time, the two of you will discuss what you have been reading in the lessons and hearing on the tapes. You will share any questions that have come to your mind about the material, and any ideas that your study has generated.

Most of the time, though, will be for the Mentor to review your progress on the exercises given for each session. This conversation should give you someone else's honest opinion about how well you are applying the principles you are studying.

Your Mentor's counsel for these three review sessions will encourage you to keep moving ahead on schedule, and to do your best possible work.

$\mathcal{U}$NIT ONE:

Laying
the Foundation

SESSION 1
God's Plan for His People

Introduction to the lesson

God loves us and wants us to love him in return. To this end we were created in his likeness — intelligent, free and holy — so that we might know him and declare his glory. Though sin ruined God's plan for our foreparents, it did not change his will for humankind. His love will not let us go. Even in his pronouncement of judgment on sinners, salvation is the reward to all who will walk in his way.

The Bible is the story of God's faithfulness to his Word, the inerrant and absolutely trustworthy account of his quest to make a people for himself, a people gathered from every tongue and tribe and nation. This is not a mere theory, or ideal, but the reality of redeemed persons living individually and together in communion with the God who loved them and gave himself for them. In New Testament language they came to be called disciples of Jesus Christ.

This first lesson will be an overview of the biblical plan for God's people in our commitment to him, in our daily walk with him, and in our witness for him.

Goals for this session

1. You will affirm that God's plan for his people is that they walk with him in holiness of life and witness to him by every way available at all times.
2. You will discover that God's plan for his people is revealed throughout Scripture.
3. You will observe how Jesus and the early church were faithful to God's plan.
4. You will commit yourself to seek to keep in step with God's plan in every aspect of your life.

As you begin...

Listen to the messages for Session One (Cassette Tape 1)

> The tapes represent excerpts from presentations by powerful speakers in the ministry of disciplemaking. The segments are intended to be a prelude to the lesson, highlighting key themes, and to be an inspiration to you as you soak up the wisdom in them. They supplement the lesson material, but do not necessarily use the same specific terms or vocabulary. Use them to set the stage for your study.

The Lesson

I. GOD'S PLAN FOR HIS PEOPLE

The Bible begins with the words "In the beginning God" (Gen. 1:1), and the rest of Scripture from Genesis to Revelation shows God at work to accomplish his purposes. Through its entirety shines the glory of his grace.

As Creator he made the universe, with the earth designed as a habitat for persons to live in fellowship with him. The first couple was told, "Be fruitful and increase in number!" (Gen. 1:28) This means not only physical reproduction, but also the care of his people's spiritual life through the sharing of the knowledge of God to succeeding generations. This is the beginning of what later is called the Great Commission.

After an unknown time, Adam and Eve turned their affection to themselves. Through the lying enticements of the devil, they disobeyed their Lord, and in that act brought sin and degradation into the human race (Gen. 3:1-19; Rom. 5:12-21). All persons thereafter have been born in iniquity and under the condemnation of God.

Yet in that most awful historic event, God's amazing grace — undeserved love — was revealed. Instead of immediate judgment came mercy and the promise of a Savior. From the seed of woman would come one who would crush the power of Satan (Gen. 3:15), bringing to humankind the means of a restored relationship.

God will not be defeated in his creation purpose. Even when the wickedness of men and women so invokes his wrath that he cannot bear their folly anymore, as with the generation of Noah and the arrogant society building the tower of Babel, he does not blot out humankind entirely.

The divine determination to make a people to praise him comes beautifully into focus in the call of Abraham to leave his home and go to a new land of promise. "I will make you into a great nation," God said, "and all peoples on earth will be blessed through you" (Gen. 12:1-3; cf. 15:1-6; 18:18; 22:18). His posterity was to become "as numerous as the stars in the sky and as countless as the sand on the seashore" (Heb. 11:12; cf. Gen. 15:5).

What was revealed to Abraham is repeated again and again to his descendants (Gen. 26:4; 28:4; Ex. 32:13; etc.). Furthermore, his seed is to become God's means of bringing "salvation to the ends of the earth" (Isa. 49:6; cf. 42:6). By their holy life, "many peoples and powerful nations" would come to see the superior nature of their God and "seek the Lord Almighty" (Zech. 8:22-23; cf. Isa. 55:4-5; Jer. 10:7).

Tragically, however, the chosen people seldom fulfill their mission in the world. More often than not they succumb to the sins of the pagans about them and have neither a witness nor a love for their neighbors. Jonah's reluctance to go and preach to Nineveh, notwithstanding the command of God, typifies in a personal way the moral disposition of Israel (Jonah 1:1 - 4:11).

Still there were occasions when the vision of God's universal family broke through their self-centeredness, as when Solomon prayed to God that "all the peoples of the earth may know your name and fear you" (I Kings 8:43, 60; 2 Chron. 6:33). The Psalmist also spoke of declaring the glory of the Lord to the nations (Psa. 97:6; 99:3-5). There were instances, too, when the prophets envisioned a day when all the ends of the earth would turn to God and be saved (Isa. 45:22; cf. 66:19), and "the earth will be filled with the knowledge of the glory of the Lord, as the waters cover the sea" (Hab. 2:14).

This future reign of blessedness was associated with the promised Messiah, to whom the Kingdom "belongs and the obedience of the nations is his" (Gen. 49:10). Through him evil will be destroyed, righteousness established and "of the increase of his government and peace there will be no end" (Isa. 9:7). These prophecies pointed to the consummation of history and the return of the triumphant King, "one like a son of man, coming with the clouds of heaven" to reign

NATIONS WILL WORSHIP HIM

over his people (Dan. 7:13). He will be "given authority, glory and sovereign power; all peoples, nations and men of every language "will worship him; and he will receive a kingdom "that will never be destroyed" (Dan. 7:14; cf. Zech. 9:10). As the chosen people of God in the world today, Christians can by God's power help fulfill his mission in the world for this generation.

II. THE MINISTRY OF CHRIST

In the fullness of time Jesus came. Everything that God had planned in the beginning was fulfilled in his Son. He made himself of no reputation, bearing our sorrows, carrying our griefs. Finally, he took on the sins of the world in his own body and offered himself as our sacrifice that we might be reconciled to God. "For God so loved the world that he gave his only Son, that whosoever believes in him shall not perish but have everlasting life." (John 3:16)

...from the East and the West...

While among us, he preached the Gospel of the Kingdom, calling all who come to him to enter into his peace through true repentance and faith. Conscious of the joy that was before him, he gladly bore the cross, "scorning its shame" (Heb. 12:2). He knew that from the nations a people would be saved through his blood. Someday they will "come from the east and the west, and will take their places at the feast with Abraham, Isaac, and Jacob in the kingdom of heaven" (Matt. 8:11). The gathering of the redeemed around the throne of God was in his thinking every time he referred to himself as the Son of Man (82 times this expression is recorded on his lips, e.g. Matt. 9:6; Luke 19:10), just as it throbbed in his heart when he spoke of the Kingdom. Recall, as an example, the last supper with his disciples, when he gave the cup to them, saying, "I will not drink of this fruit of the vine from now on until that day when I drink it anew with you in my Father's kingdom" (Matt. 26:29; cf.

Mark 14:25). Visions of that destined union filled his mind with glory; it flooded his soul even as he prayed on the eve of Calvary (John 17:5, 24). As a Christian, one of the greatest thoughts you have is that final vision, that final union with Christ. Right? Then, let's help others who need to become a disciple of Christ; share that vision!

He knew, of course, before the nations could bow at his feet this good news of his finished work must be made known to the ends of the earth. In its ultimate realization, then, the coming of Christ and his Kingdom awaits the evangelization of the world. Only after the Gospel has been preached in all the world as a witness can the end to which history is moving come (Matt. 24:14). It is not difficult to understand why Jesus gave such force to the Great Commission after his resurrection and before ascending into the heavens to assume his place of authority at the right hand of the Majesty on High.

REVIEW BEFORE YOU GO AHEAD

1. Answer the following true-or-false questions by writing T or F in the blank spaces which corresponds to the question:

___ The Bible unfolds around man's quest for God, not God's quest for man.

___ The Great Commission begins with God's design in creation.

___ God will not be defeated in his purpose to make a people for himself.

___ God's plan to raise up a people from every nation can be seen in Abraham's call.

___ The Kingdom is where Christ reigns as King.

___ The Kingdom comes through humanitarian service by raising our standard of living.

2. Why is the preaching of the Gospel so crucial to God's plan for the world?

3. What will happen after the Gospel is preached to the ends of the world?

III. PEOPLE WITH A MISSION

All four of the Gospel writers record the glorified Lord charging his disciples with the task of reaching the world with the good news of salvation, and each relates it with an unique perspective. The various commissions restate for a new generation God's redemptive plan through the ages.

Matthew presents Christ telling his followers: "All authority in heaven and on earth has been given to me. Therefore go and make disciples of all nations, baptizing them in the name of the Father and of the Son and of the Holy Spirit, and teaching them to obey everything I have commanded you. And surely I am with you always, to the very end of the age" (Matt. 28:18-20). The term "go" here literally means "as you go," signifying that disciplemaking is to be a part of our lifestyle wherever we are.

Jesus Christ is Lord!

Mark 16:15 in Action

Mark frames the commission in the words of Jesus, "Go into all the world and preach the good news to all creation" (Mark 16:15). The accent is upon the necessity of taking initiative and verbally proclaiming the Gospel. The verb "preach" is an imperative, expressing an urgent command to herald the message of the One who sends. It should be understood that the preaching described here is not limited to formal delivery associated with a pulpit ministry. The manner and style of speaking depends upon the situation. What matters is that the message gets to every living creature. In this task every believer is a herald of Christ.

Luke, in both the Gospel and the Book of Acts, uses the term "witness." Jesus, on the first Easter Sunday, told his disciples, "This is what is written: The Christ will suffer and rise from the dead on the third day, and repentance and forgiveness of sins will be preached in his name to all nations, beginning at Jerusalem. You are witnesses of these things" (Luke 24:46-48). In another record Luke notes Jesus' final words, "You will be my *witnesses*" (Acts 1:8). Witnessing means to bear testimony to what is known personally to be true (I John 1:1). It includes more than talking, though what we believe should find expression in our speech. Witnessing incarnates the reality of the message in the person giving it.

John records the simple statement of Jesus: "Peace be with you! As the Father has sent me, I am sending you" (John 20:21; cf. John 17:18). Here the emphasis is upon the missionary nature of the Commission. The similarity between our Lord's controlling sense of mission and that of his disciples cannot be mistaken. Just as he was sent by the Father to carry out God's purposes — a work now accomplished — so those who believe on him receive apostleship and are sent forth in his name. It is well to observe, too, the incarnational dimension of the mission. Christ had to renounce his own rights and take the form of a servant when he was sent into the world. In the same way, his disciples become an embodiment of the message they bear and live in the world as the Lord set an example.

The *plan* of God the Father, the *commission* of God the Son and the *power* of God the Holy Spirit call all of us to be obedient servants. Today more than ever people in the world around us are searching for meaning in life. They need God's presence and power in their lives. Our mission is to assist them in their search, ultimately for a personal relationship with God through Jesus Christ.

As You Go, Make Disciples Everywhere

Home   Work

School   Recreation

IV. THE CHURCH IN ACTION

The Book of Acts shows how the early followers of Christ took to heart their Lord's command to make Christ known to the world. They not only "filled Jerusalem" with their teaching (Acts 5:28), they "preached the word wherever they went" (Acts 8:4). Whether at

Clergy Leadership

home or abroad on missionary journeys, these believers went about witnessing to others.

However, as the church grew an unfortunate clergy/laity distinction began to develop. By the fourth century ministry largely had been relegated to an ordained priesthood. The laity were expected to do what the clergy told them to do, a role which they passively accepted. This development was surely one of Satan's greatest victories, for it had the effect of immobilizing 95% of the church.

To show how things can get turned around, the word "clergy" comes from a Greek word "cleros" which translates heir or inheritance, and when used in reference to the church in the New Testament refers to every born again believer (e.g. Rom. 8:17; Acts 20:32). On the other hand, the word "laity" comes from a Greek term "laos," meaning people. Both words, then, indicate that ministry belongs to *every* member of the body of Christ.

Clearly God expects all his people to carry out his mission. Persons who are in leadership roles in the church are responsible to make sure that believers understand this and are equipped for ministry.

"It was he [God] who gave some to be apostles, some to be prophets, some to be evangelists, and some to be pastors and teachers, to prepare God's people for works of service, so that the body of Christ may be built up" (Eph. 4:11-12).

Clergy/ Laity Leadership

This is a key point to note. Gifted leaders in evangelism and discipling, like pastors and teachers, are not to do all the work of the ministry. Rather, they are to train the congregation for the ministry which they share together.

Look also at 2 Corinthians 5:17–6:2. You will observe that all persons who have been created new in Christ (vs. 17) are given "the ministry of reconciliation" (vs. 18). We are "Christ's ambassadors, as though God were making his appeal through us" (vs. 20). It can be summarized as follows:

(1) We join God in his quest to fill the earth with his glory.
(2) We go on this mission with the reality of Christ's saving work in our lives.
(3) All believers have the authority of Christ to do his ministry.
(4) God's plan is to bring the Gospel to every person on the earth.
(5) God's mission methods are sharing the gospel, making disciples, assimilating people into local fellowship groups and teaching them to reproduce spiritually.
(6) We know Jesus is with us in all aspects of his mission.
(7) God's mission continues until he calls us to himself or until Jesus comes again.

REVIEW BEFORE YOU GO AHEAD

1. Answer the following true-or-false questions by writing T or F in the blank spaces which corresponds to the question:

___ God's plan for evangelizing the world is that it takes place through his redeemed people.

___ The Holy Trinity is involved in Christian ministry.

___ The professional clergy are called by God to do all the work of the church.

2. What is the dominant emphasis of each of the Commissions?

Matthew

Mark

Luke

John

3. Think about the clergy/laity distinction. Describe in terms of actual ministry what this has done in your church.

V. THE RESULTANT PEACE

To enter into the ministry with God we must learn to walk with him. Many action words are used to describe this walk: **Fear** (reverence) the Lord, **love** the Lord, **obey** the Lord, **cling** to the Lord, **keep** the commandments of the Lord, and **serve** the Lord. It can be summarized in an easy to remember acrostic: **F - L - O - C - K - S**.

When we are walking with God there is always peace. We often think of peace as the absence of war among nations or tensions among people. But the Hebrew word "shalom" has a more powerful meaning. This peace has in it the inherent idea of harmony in all directions and all relationships. Additionally, it is to be eternal: "We have peace with God" (Rom. 5:1).

The Christian lives in the joy of the Lord. There is a beautiful inward assurance of salvation. And "the peace of God, which transcends all understanding, will guard your hearts and your minds in Christ Jesus" (Phil. 4:7).

Witnessing in daily fellowship with Christ to others is simply the overflow of a close communion with Jesus. That is why it is essential that every Christian learn to dwell in the presence of the Lord. Lorne Sanny, former President of the Navigators, often would tell his audiences, "Take a good look at Jesus Christ, then tell others what you saw." D.T. Niles of India once defined witnessing as "one beggar telling another beggar where to find bread."

One of the best ways to maintain this fellowship is to keep a daily devotional time or "Quiet Time" with God. Because this time with the Lord brings so much spiritual vitality into our lives we can expect the devil to do everything possible to hinder it. If you have found this true in your life, the suggestions for keeping a Quiet Time in Appendix A will be helpful.

The peace that we know in our witness for God and our walk with him now is but a preview of what is to come. For we know that when we have done the will of God in this life, our Lord will say to us at the end of the way, "Well done, good and faithful servant!" (Matt. 25:21).

When you are weary in the work, think of the vision John had of that "great multitude" of the faithful witnesses at the throne of heaven: "They were wearing white robes and were holding palm branches in their hands." Their number is so great that "no one can count them." As far as the eye can see, in every direction, from the east and the west, from the north and the south, they are gathered. They came "from every nation, tribe, people and language" (Rev. 7:9). The Great Commission is fulfilled! With mighty acclamation they cry, "Salvation belongs to our God, who sits on the throne, and to the Lamb" (Rev. 7:10). God's ultimate plan for his people is to joyously serve and praise him without ceasing.

And as John beheld the Holy City prepared as a bride adorned for her husband, he heard a loud voice from the throne saying, "Now the dwelling of God is with men, and he will live with them. They will be his people, and God himself will be with them and be their God" (Rev. 21:3).

That is reality! That is eternity. And the whole renewed creation will be at peace, the plan of God accomplished.

A CLOSING CHALLENGE

This lesson has introduced the plan of God for his world and his people. Salvation by grace through faith is God's design from beginning to end. God himself is the ultimate evangelist. Part of that process is God's call to redeemed men and women to walk with him in holiness of life, committing themselves to the lordship of Christ and submitting to the Holy Spirit so that he can fill and empower them for ministry (Eph. 5:18).

You cannot minister to others in evangelism, follow-up, or discipling without being a disciple of Jesus Christ yourself. If that is the case, then it just could be that you will have to start changes in your life. You may have to set aside some habits that are not pleasing to the Lord and begin to develop new patterns of behavior. You may need to renew your love to Christ. You cannot give what you do not have any more than you can come back from some place you have never been. Therefore, the challenge of this first lesson is to personally make sure that you...

(1) be in his plan for your life;

(2) commit yourself to growing in your Christian faith by walk-ing with him every day,

(3) are determined as a result of your daily walk with him to be a consistent witness for Jesus for the praise of his glory.

THE BELIEVER'S WALK WITH GOD AND WITNESS FOR GOD

Walk   *Witness*

BELIEVER   **UNBELIEVER**

♦ *Ideas to Remember*

Almighty God has a determined plan for his creation, and that plan includes his highest order of creation — humanity. God created us in his own image that we might have fellowship with him and glorify him forever. In discovering God's plan for his world and for our lives, we have noted the following key ingredients:

♦ God is both Creator and Redeemer.

♦ Christians are to walk with God daily in obedience.

♦ Believers are to witness for Christ, carrying out his redemp-tive mission in this world.

♦ Faithful witnesses continually are to experience God's peace.

Application of the Lesson

1. Examine your relationship with Jesus Christ. Are you following him or living *your* way? Check the following areas of your life in which you know that Christ is in control.

    ❐ Relationships at home   ❐ Time
    ❐ Finances   ❐ Thoughts
    ❐ Business activities   ❐ Speech
    ❐ Priorities   ❐ Friendships
    ❐ Recreation   ❐ Career

2. Look at the items you did not check in question #1 and write out what you can do to place this area under God's control.

3. In the lesson we discussed the acrostic **F-L-O-C-K-S**. Evaluate the level of your obedience to each of these commands:

	most of the time	sometimes	hardly ever
Fear [reverence] the Lord	❐	❐	❐
Love the Lord	❐	❐	❐
Obey the Lord	❐	❐	❐
Cling to the Lord	❐	❐	❐
Keep His commandments	❐	❐	❐
Serve the Lord	❐	❐	❐

4. Are you using any of the following excuses to sidestep your responsibility to be a witness for Jesus Christ?

    ❐ "I'm afraid"   ❐ "That's the pastor's job"
    ❐ "I don't care"   ❐ "I'm not good enough"
    ❐ "I'm too busy"   ❐ "I'm not eloquent"
    ❐ "I don't know how"   ❐ "I haven't been to seminary"

What will you do about it?

5. Memorize Romans 3:23 and Romans 6:23 in a Bible version of your choice or language.

   **(See Appendix B for helpful information on
   how to memorize Scripture)**

S ESSION 2
The Ministry of Christ

Introduction to the lesson

An ancient story records a conversation Jesus had with angels after his return to heaven. Acting as the spokesperson, the Archangel Gabriel asked Jesus what he had been doing on Earth.

Jesus told the large group of angels that he had lived as a real human, that he had died on a cross to save humanity from its sins, that he had been raised from the dead by the power of God, and that he had now made it possible for the world to be saved. He concluded by saying that it was his desire that all humans everywhere in all generations hear the message of what he had done for them and that they come into his kingdom.

Gabriel asked, "And what is your plan for getting this done?"

Jesus replied, "Oh, I left the message in the hands of my disciples. They will pass on the word to others."

Somewhat surprised, Gabriel exclaimed, "But what if they fail?"

Jesus declared, "I have no other plan. I am counting on them!"

Despite the legendary nature of this conversation, the main point of it is true. Jesus *did* leave the task of evangelizing the whole world in the hands of a few men and women who trusted him. Following the coming of the Holy Spirit in power on the Day of Pentecost, this group of committed disciples within a generation turned the Roman world "upside down" (Acts 17:6, NKJV). We believe in Christ today because of the commitment and faithfulness of these early disciples.

Jesus' plan, confirming what God had purposed from "before the foundation of the world" (Eph. 1:4, NASB) and had carried out throughout the Old Testament,

God's Task for Mankind

has never changed. The world has changed; technology has altered society; programs have become more sophisticated; but the plan of God has not changed. Redemption has always been by grace through faith; the call of God to his own has always been to walk with him and to serve him by being a witness to the ends of the earth.

How did Jesus train his disciples to carry on his ministry? This lesson seeks to answer that question. The assumption is that Jesus followed the most effective way of discipling. If there had been a better way, he would have used it. It is, therefore, necessary for believers of every generation to know the pattern of Jesus' ministry, and to apply it to their culture and age. This is our challenge as well.

Goals for this session

1. You will distinguish between Jesus' public and private ministry.
2. You will discern his pattern of ministry in training others to be spiritual reproducers.
3. You will glean transferable principles of his ministry and make them your own.
4. You will begin practicing Jesus' methods in your own ministry.

As you begin...

Listen to the messages for Session Two (Cassette Tape 1)

The Lesson

Many students of the Bible research the Gospels to find what Jesus did in his ministry of preaching, teaching, healing, and performing miracles. Careful study uncovers many tremendous principles of ministry that apply cross-culturally and across time.

I. THE MANNER OF JESUS' MINISTRY

Jesus often ministered to the multitudes; scripture denotes at least 17 instances. We see him surrounded by crowds as he taught. He set forth information about God, his love, his salvation, and our necessary response to him. We see large groups of people flocking to witness his miracles and healing ministry.

The bulk of his time, however, was spent not in public ministry with vast multitudes of people, but in private with his disciples, as recorded approximately 46 times in the Bible. There he trained his committed followers for their own ministries. Sometimes Jesus ministered one-on-one [approximately 28 times] (Matt. 9:9-11; Luke 19:1-28; John 1:43; 3:1-21; 4:6-26, etc.); at other times Jesus trained one-on-two or one-on-three (Mark 5:35-42); at other times his ministry was conducted one-on-twelve (Matt. 10:1-5a). He also did some on-the-job training with 70 (Luke 10:1-24); he spent some apprenticeship time with the 120 on whom the Spirit would come on the Day of Pentecost (Acts 1:15b); and he must have had some input to the 500 in Galilee (1 Cor. 15:6 with Matt. 28:16-20).

The training was similar to what today's surgeons receive when they are trained by a skilled, more experienced doctor; or when pilots-to-be are trained by a skilled, older pilot. This *apprenticeship* was the type of in-depth training that Jesus had in mind when he commanded his followers to "go and make disciples of all nations, baptizing them in the name of the Father, and of the Son and of the Holy Spirit, and teaching them to obey everything I have commanded you..." (Matt. 28:19-20).

In the original text, there is but one verb, "*make* disciples." "Go," "baptizing," and "teaching" are participles, which means that these activities do not stand alone. As in English, so in Greek: participles derive their force from the leading verb. The implications of this are quite significant for ministry — the reason for going anywhere, whether next door or across the ocean, is to make disciples. *The whole thrust of the Great Commission — giving direction and validity to every effort — is the discipling of all nations.*

Notice that the command is not to make converts and stop there. In other contexts, of course, Jesus emphasizes the necessity of conversion (e.g. Matt. 18:3; John 3:1-36). Tragically, however, many "converts" fail to go on with Jesus, and his plan for reaching the world through their witness never comes to fruition. The irresponsible way that the church as a whole has accommodated this situation explains why so much of the world's population still languishes in darkness.

Disciple

A *disciple* means "learner or pupil," as in the sense of an apprentice. Such a person is more than a convert, though turning to the Savior in repentance and faith certainly must take place. But disciples do not stop with con-

Decision Only

version; they keep moving on with Christ, ever learning more about how to live like him daily.

Here is the genius of his plan to win "all nations," raising up a people in his likeness. For disciples of Christ grow in his character, and by the same virtue, they develop in his life-style and ministry to the world. By making this the focal concern, Jesus assures an ever-enlarging labor force, and in time, through multiplication, workers will bring the good news to the ends of the earth.

Christ's disciples are only asked to live by the same rule that governed his time among us. That is what the commission is all about. It simply enunciates the strategy implicit in his own ministry while he was with us in the flesh. Just as the Lord ordered his life on earth, now his disciples are expected to follow in his steps.

II. THE PATTERN OF JESUS' MINISTRY

To understand the pattern of Jesus' ministry, we must look closely at the way Jesus made disciples. His pattern of disciplemaking becomes the interpretation of the command.

Adaptations of his approach to ministry, of course, must be made to our situation. The techniques Christ used in his culture, nearly twenty centuries ago, are not necessarily the same techniques he would use in our situation today. Methods are variable, conditioned by the time

Growing to Be More Like Christ

and circumstances, which are constantly changing. But principles, inherent in his way of life, never change. They provide guidelines for making disciples in every society and every age.

1. Servanthood — *Jesus Lived as a Servant (Matt. 20:28)*

One does not have to observe Jesus very long without being made aware that he lived by a different value system from that of the world. Renouncing his own rights, he "made himself nothing, taking the very nature of a servant, being made in human likeness" (Phil. 2:7).

Most of his incarnate life was lived in obscurity in an unbe-coming city, where he learned a carpenter's trade. At about the age of thirty, having fulfilled the obligations of the eldest son, Jesus left home to pursue his public career. He was then accosted by Satan and tempted with the allurements of the world. "Get what you deserve — turn stones into bread to satisfy your appetite, then jump off the pinnacle of the temple that the angels of God might lift you up," the archdeceiver taunted (*see* Matt. 4:1-7; Luke 4:1-4; 9-13). How these feats of power would have invoked the crowd's applause! In fact, Jesus was promised all the kingdoms of the earth, if he would only accommodate "the god of this age" (Matt. 4:8-10; 2 Cor. 4:4). But our Lord would not be diverted from his mission; his work cannot be accomplished by indulgence of the flesh, however legitimate the appeal.

Jesus came to serve, and in that role he went about doing good. Little wonder that multitudes were drawn to him. People always respond to love, when it finds practical expression in ministry, the more so when it is empowered by the Spirit of God. Though his fearless preaching often invoked the disdain of the religious gentry, it generally was received with appreciation by the masses (Mark 12:12; Matt. 21:26; Luke 20:19). Indicative of his popular following, the last time he entered Jerusalem, crowds turned out to welcome him, shouting, "'Hosanna! Blessed is he who comes in the name of the Lord.'" (John 12:13).

We must ask ourselves the question, "Are others drawn to me because of my love for them so I can then tell them about Christ?"

2. Selection — *Jesus Looked for Disciples (Luke 6:13)*

But as Jesus looked upon the city, tears filled his eyes, for he knew that the people did not really understand who he was, nor did they comprehend the Kingdom that he had come to establish (Luke 19:41-44). They were lost like sheep without a shepherd to lead in the way of God. Jesus was doing all he could to help, but in the incarnation, he assumed the limitation of his body. He could not give attention to all the people. Unless spiritual leaders could be raised up who could multiply his ministry — redeemed men and women with the heart of Christ — there was no way the waiting harvest could be gathered (Matt. 9:37,38).

So while ministering to the multitudes, Jesus concentrated upon making some disciples who would learn to reproduce his life and mission. In doing so he loved the multitudes no less. Indeed, it was for the sake of the masses that he had to devote himself to a few willing learners in order for the world ultimately to be reached.

His first disciples were found largely within his home environment in Galilee. In culture, training, and religious orientation they had much in common. To be sure, they were not generally the most socially astute people, perhaps not even the most religious. None of them, for example, appear to be members of the Levitical priesthood. By any standard of sophisticated culture, they would be viewed as a rather unpromising aggregation of souls.

Yet Jesus saw in these untrained laymen the potential for turning the world upside down. In spite of their limitations, they were willing to follow Jesus. That is all he asked (John 1:43,46; Mark 2:14; Matt. 4:19,20; 9:9; Luke 5:27). Though often superficial in their comprehension of spiritual reality, with the exception of the traitor, they were teachable. Such persons can be molded into a new image.

3. Association — *Jesus Stayed with His Learners (Mark 3:14)*

As their numbers grew, Jesus appointed twelve to be "with him" in a special apostleship (Mark 3:14). He continued to relate to others as the fellowship of believers increased through his ministry, but it is apparent that he gave a diminishing priority of attention to those outside the apostolic circle. In this select group, Peter, James, and John seemed to enjoy an even closer relationship to the Master.

Do you see the deliberate way that Jesus invested his life in a few persons whom he was training? His approach illustrates a basic principle of teaching: the more concentrated the size of the group being taught, the greater the opportunity for learning. In a profound sense, he is showing us how the Great Commission can become the controlling purpose of every family circle, every small group gathering, every close friendship in this life.

For the better part of three years, Jesus stayed with his pupils. Together they walked the highways and streets; together they sailed on the lake; together they visited friends; together they went to the synagogue and the temple; together they worked. Have you noticed that he seldom did anything alone? Imagine! He came to save the nations — and finally, he died on the cross for all humankind. Yet while here he spent more time with a handful of disciples than with everybody else in the world. You too can invest your life in a quality way in one, two or a few others.

4. Consecration — *Jesus Expected Obedience (John 14:23)*

Jesus called people to obedience. They were not required to be smart, but they had to follow him. Obedience is the action of faith and the manifestation of love: "If you love me," he taught, "you will obey what I command" (John 14:15).

What is more, obedience is the means of learning more truth. Jesus taught that choosing to do God's will was a condition for further illumination of truth (John 7:17).

Not surprisingly, then, his early followers were known as disciples, or his pupils. It was not until much later that they started to be called "Christians" (Acts 11:16), although it was inevitable, for in time consistent followers take on the character of their leader. In calling them to obedience, Jesus simply was reflecting his own submission to the Father: "I always do what pleases him" (John 8:29). Stop for a moment and think, "Am I obedient to him, a true follower of Christ? In what ways? How could I improve?"

5. Demonstration — *Jesus Showed Them How to Minister (John 13:15)*

In this close association, the disciples were given a demonstration of his mission. His life was the *object lesson* of his doctrine. By practicing before them what he wanted them to learn, they could see its relevance and application.

Take, for example, his habit of prayer. Surely it was no accident that Jesus often let his disciples see him conversing with the Father. They could observe the priority of this spiritual discipline and the strength it gave to his life. Inevitably the time came when they asked him, "Lord, teach us to pray..." (Luke 11:1). They were ready to learn. Notice, though, in this beginning lesson, he did not preach them a sermon or assign them a book to read; he gave them an example (Luke 11:2-4; Matt. 6:9-13).

In the same way, he taught his disciples the importance and use of Scripture, the meaning of worship, stewardship of time and talents, social responsibility, and every other aspect of his personal life. All the while, of course, he was showing them how to care for the needs of people, bearing their sorrows, carrying their grief, ever seeking their ultimate welfare in the gospel. In the process he was also demonstrating how to make disciples.

6. Delegation — *Jesus Involved His Disciples in Ministry* (Luke 10:1)

As they were able to assume responsibility, he involved them in activities suited to their gifts. First duties were small, unassuming tasks, like providing for the food and shelter of the group. After a while he began to have the disciples assist him in ministry. They were employed, for example, in baptizing persons who responded to his preaching (John 4:2). In another setting, he has them distributing food to hungry people who came to hear him (Mark 6:30-44; 18:1-9; Matt. 14:13-21; 15:29-38; Luke 9:10-17; John 6:1-13).

The work assignments increased with their developing self-confidence and competence. Before long they were sent out to do much the same kind of work that Jesus was doing with them — healing, teaching, and preaching the gospel (Matt. 10:1-10; Mark 6:6-13; Luke 9:1-3; cf. 10:1-16). Lest they forget the priority of training leadership, however, he stipulated that above the public ministry they were to search out "worthy" persons to spend time with, wherever they went (Matt. 10:11-15; Mark 6:10,11; Luke 9:4,5). In effect, the disciples were told to concentrate upon the most promising people, who would be able to follow up their ministry after they were gone.

7. Supervision — *Jesus Made His Disciples Accountable* (Luke 10:17)

From time to time Jesus would get back with them and see how things were coming along. He would check up on their assignments, ask questions, and respond to their queries. He was building in them a sense of accountability. Experiences the disciples were having in ministry thus became illustrations for him to teach some new or deeper truth (e.g. Luke 9:37-43; 10:14-24; Matt. 15:37-16:12; 17:14-20; Mark 8:10-21; 9:17-29). It was on-the-job training all the way.

Problems were dealt with as they came up, which was quite often. Certainly the disciples were far from perfection, and their spiritual immaturity was constantly coming out. To note one instance, recall the time James and John wanted to call down fire on the heads of some disrespectful Samaritans who refused them shelter (Luke 9:51-56). When Jesus saw their impulsiveness, he rebuked them but also seized the occasion to emphasize again the saving purpose of his mission. "You do not know what kind of spirit you are of, for the Son of Man did not come to destroy men's lives, but to save them" (Luke 9:55-56).

The need for accountability between Christians is very important in the church today. Through a discipling process, which this course will explain, one can lovingly confront and encourage a brother or sister who is wrong.

8. Reproduction—*Jesus Trained His Disciples to Multiply Spiritually (John 15:16)*

Life inevitably reproduces its own kind. Careless persons who let the lusts of this world choke the Word of God will reap the folly of their ways. Weak, undisciplined Christians will produce weak, undisciplined offspring, not true disciples. On the other hand, those living in conformity to Christ's Word develop the qualities of his life and ministry — our goal.

His parable of the vine and the branches is a beautiful illustration (John 15:1-17). Jesus likens himself in this analogy to the vine and his disciples to the branches. The branches are conveyors of the life in the vine and, when properly functioning, produce a harvest. Any branch not fulfilling its purpose is cut off. Even producing branches are pruned by the gardener in order that they will be more fruitful.

When fruit bearing is seen in this larger context of producing Christ-likeness, first in ourselves and then in others, practically everything Jesus did and said pointed to this truth. The Great Commission simply brings the principle into focus, phrasing it in terms of disciplemaking.

Jesus taught his followers to live with the harvest in view. "...Open your eyes and look at the fields!" he said, noticing the men coming to hear him in Sychar, "They are ripe for harvest" (John 4:36). The disciples could see what he meant and could also appreciate its spiritual application when he added, "Even now the reaper draws his wages, even now he harvests the crop for eternal life..." (John 4:36). Whether they sowed or reaped, he wanted the disciples to realize that their work had impact upon eternity, ultimately culminating in the gathering of the nations at the throne of God. Today our lives as disciples of Christ have that same impact as we produce disciples.

The key to the final harvest is found in the quality and the supply of laborers obeying the mandate of Christ. It does not matter how few their numbers are in the beginning, provided that they reproduce and teach their disciples in turn to do the same. As simple as it may seem, this is the way his church will ultimately triumph. He has no other plan.

REVIEW BEFORE YOU GO AHEAD

1. Answer the following true-or-false questions by writing T or F in the blank space which corresponds to the question:

___ (a) Jesus trained in depth thousands of disciples.

___ (b) Jesus spent more time in private ministry to his disciples than he did in public ministry to the multitudes.

___ (c) Jesus has entrusted to angels the task of sharing the Gospel with the whole world.

___ (d) Jesus expected his original disciples to reproduce and train others to reproduce as well.

___ (e) Jesus' disciples had little time with him personally.

2. Thinking through Jesus' pattern in making disciples, put in your own words the eight unchanging principles that have been discussed:

1) _____   5) _____

2) _____   6) _____

3) _____   7) _____

4) _____   8) _____

3. Which of the 8 principles in Jesus' ministry do you feel is the *strongest* in your ministry?

_____

Which is the *weakest*?

_____

What changes do you need to make in order to strengthen that principle in your life and ministry?

_____

_____

_____

III. A PATTERN FOR OUR MINISTRY

He has given us a model that in principle every believer can follow. Too easily we have relegated his work to organized programs and special clerical vocations. Not that these ministries are unnecessary — indeed they are vital! But unless the Great Commission directs the daily life of the whole body, the church cannot function as it should. Besides, there are simply not enough professional clergy to do all the work where you live, work and play.

Here the priesthood of all believers comes alive. Whatever our place of service, we live with a sense of destiny, knowing that each day moves us closer to consummation of the Kingdom. Making disciples is not a special calling or a gift of the Spirit; it is a lifestyle — the way that Jesus lived while he was among us and now the way he commands his people to follow.

♦ *Begin Where You Are*

Since disciplemaking is best accomplished with a few people at any one time, you will never lack an opportunity for ministry. You may be sure, too, that some of those who feel the warmth of your servant heart will also want to know more about your Lord. Notice them. They are the answer to your prayers.

If you look around, you will see persons with whom you already have much in common, beginning with your own family and reaching out from there to neighbors and friends. Within this natural sphere of influence, you will probably have the greatest potential for changing the world.

With those persons who do not yet know the Savior, your relationship becomes a means of clarifying the gospel, bringing them to a place of decision. The same servanthood pertains to believers needing encouragement and direction in their Christian life. Though you are not the only person responsible for their discipleship, you may be, for a period of time, one of the most significant influences in their Christian growth.

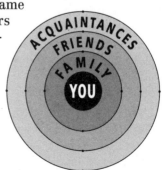

Relationships in your Ministry

◆ Learning Family Style

Like Jesus, you disciple by being together. The more informal the association the better, like traveling together or engaging in some form of recreational activity. What practical ways to have meaningful conversations! Such casual activities, of course, do not take the place of formal church services. Both are needed and serve the same purpose of making disciples. But learning comes more naturally in relaxed, family-like settings.

Some of this fellowship can be arranged in small-group meetings. These periods incorporate times of testimony, Bible study, prayer, or anything else deemed important to the participants.

Such close association is especially crucial in preserving the fruit of evangelism. Like newborns in the physical world, beginning disciples must have spiritual guardians to help them in their Christian growth. Meet with them as often as possible, inquire about their needs, answer their questions, encourage their witness, and make them feel a part of the body of Christ.

◆ Give Disciples Something to Do

Maturing disciples may find they want to get involved in ministry by helping to follow-up a new believer. Many of the programs of the church also afford opportunities for service. Early assignments can be in areas where they are already equipped, perhaps helping in the nursery or driving a bus. As they grow in grace and knowledge, disciples may assume leadership roles in the Sunday-school or youth activities, possibly eventually becoming deacons or elders of the congregation.

According to their gifts and level of ability, *all believers can do something.* When it comes to the Lord's work, *there is a place for everyone.* Best of all, whatever form your ministry takes, be it structured or informal, whether in the church or out in the marketplace, it is a way to help a few daring ones get involved in making disciples. When the Great Commission is seen as a life-style, nothing becomes insignificant, and everything that happens helps us know more of the grace of God.

◆ Never Stop Learning

Whatever has been experienced thus far, there is more to learn. Keeping disciples pressing on is not easy. Anyone trying to help others is sure to face frustration. As someone has said, "Ministry would be easy, if it were not for people." Innumerable things can happen to sidetrack the best of intentions, and unless these matters are faced realistically, young disciples can easily become defeated. Persist in checking up. Ask how they are coming along. Sharing out of your experiences may encourage greater openness, as well as show your own accountability.

Probably the most deceiving problems in human relations come out when the ego is offended, giving rise to various expressions of self-centeredness, such as pride or bitterness. When you recognize one of these fleshly traits, you must help the disciple bring it to the cross. Rebuke will not be resented when given in love, especially if we build self-esteem in them through consistent commendation of every evidence of progress in the disciple's developing priesthood.

Giving this kind of leadership puts us on the spot. Perhaps that is why we have such difficulty equipping disciples, for it means that we must be prepared to have them follow us, even as we follow the Lord (1 Cor. 11:1).

It makes us vulnerable, of course. Persons whom we let into the inner workings of our lives will surely see our shortcomings and failures. But let them also see a readiness to confess our sins when we understand the error of our ways. Let them hear us apologize to those we have wronged. Weaknesses need not impair discipleship when there is transparent sincerity to follow Christ. An honest exposure may tarnish our halo, but in seeing our humanness, others may more easily identify with our precepts. Furthermore, if we learn from our failures, as abundant as they are, there is no end to the lessons we'll derive.

Though we are witnesses, let us *make clear that Christ is the authority, not ourselves.* Avoid any authoritarian role of a master guru. Jesus alone commands. In subjection to him, discipler and disciple together learn at his feet.

♦ *Leave With a Vision*

Aided by your example, those persons close to you will begin to realize how Christ has ordered your steps. Now you can specifically share your philosophy of ministry with them. They will be able to understand, for in some measure they will have seen its interpretation in your investment in them.

You can dream together about their place in the harvest and how God will use their unique personalities and gifts in ways far beyond your own. As they get their vision focused, encourage them to set some goals for the future as to where they would like to be ten, twenty, thirty years hence. With these projections in view, the next step is to help them map out plans to achieve their aims. It is in these hours of dreaming that a long-term strategy of discipling really takes shape.

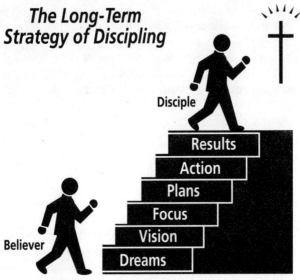

The Long-Term Strategy of Discipling

Disciple

Results
Action
Plans
Focus
Vision
Dreams

Believer

Every step is important. No step can be left out.

The time will come, as with all physical relationships, when it will be necessary to withdraw from an active role in their lives. Bonds of love, though, will remain and perhaps even deepen. As they move on, others will take their place, and the process begins again. With each succeeding spiritual generation, anticipation of the harvest grows, looking joyously to the day when disciples will be made of all nations.

♦ The Call to Prayer

The greatest expression of this vision will be seen in our prayers. It is here, in communion with the Spirit of Christ, that we enter most deeply into that love which drove him into the world and now constrains us to beseech "the Lord of the harvest...to send out workers into his harvest field" (Matt. 9:38).

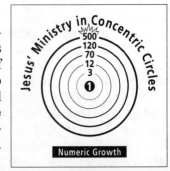

Jesus' Ministry in Concentric Circles

500
120
70
12
3
❶

Numeric Growth

Indeed, this was Christ's first missionary command. Whatever we do begins as we wait on our knees before the throne of grace.

Jesus calls his disciples to get priorities in order. To pray is to confess our own utter inability to do anything in our own strength. At the same time, it is an affirmation that God is able; nothing is too hard for him. As he commands, so he provides.

♦ *Ideas to Remember*

Our Lord did not come in his incarnate body to evangelize the world; he came to make it possible for the world to be saved through his atoning sacrifice. But on his way to Calvary, he made sure that his disciples were equipped by strategy and vision to gather the harvest. His ministry gives us the following action paths:

- ❐ How to have a meaningful relationship with God

- ❐ How to walk with him

- ❐ How to have an import private ministry in addition to a public ministry

- ❐ How to carry out a ministry of training disciples

- ❐ How to witness for him effectively

- ❐ How to reproduce

Completing all of the above depend on a right relationship with God through Christ and full dependence on the power of the Holy Spirit for ministry.

Application of the Lesson

As you consider the pattern of Jesus' ministry, test yourself as to past achievement in these principles:

	frequently	sometimes	seldom	never
1. I tell other people about Christ with a view to win them to him.	❏	❏	❏	❏
2. I attempt to assist believers in becoming more mature in their Christian lives.	❏	❏	❏	❏
3. I spend time with a few persons with whom I develop a discipling lifestyle.	❏	❏	❏	❏
4. I find ways to involve disciples in some form of ministry.	❏	❏	❏	❏
5. I keep check on these disciples and expect accountability.	❏	❏	❏	❏
6. I hold up these disciples in my prayers.	❏	❏	❏	❏

7. If not already memorized, learn Matt. 9:35-38; 28:18-20 in a Bible version of your choice or language.

SESSION 3
Empowered by the Spirit

Introduction to the lesson

Imagine a statistician trying to determine the probability of the disciples' success in influencing their world for Christ. With just a handful of uneducated, unimpressive members, this ragged band was given the task of taking the Gospel to the ends of the earth. These people were not exactly the type of individuals that looked like world-changers. Given all the factors that weighed against them, how could they possibly succeed? And yet succeed they did. They were referred to as those who had "turned the world upside down" (Acts 17:6, KJV).

What was the *secret* of their success? ***They imitated Jesus!*** The early church believers received and applied the power of the indwelling Holy Spirit and followed Jesus' strategy for ministry.

In many cultures of the world children play the game of follow the leader. One child is selected to lead, and the whole group then does exactly as the leader does. In more negative language, if one copies another person exactly, he or she is called a "copy cat." In essence, the Early Church "copycatted" Jesus. In principle they did things as he had given them an example.

The pattern is never outmoded. From the first century to the present, we find that whenever the church moved forward and was effective, it followed Jesus' pat-tern. Whenever the church abandoned Jesus' pattern, it stagnated or went backwards. The lessons of the Book of Acts, the ministry of the early church, and the record are quite clear: Jesus' way of ministry works!

In this lesson we will examine the power of the Holy Spirit at work in the early church and throughout church history, the obedience of a people or church, the role of the "layperson" in the history of redemption, and the situation today worldwide.

FOLLOW ME!

Jesus' Pattern of Ministry

Goals for this session

1. You will realize that the pattern taught and modeled by Jesus really works.
2. You will study the example of the early church as they followed Jesus' pattern.
3. You will recognize the absolute necessity of being empowered by the Holy Spirit for effective ministry.
4. You will understand the promise of revival among God's people.

As you begin...

Listen to the messages for Session Three (Cassette Tape 1)

The Lesson

Reading the Book of Acts will show that despite seemingly insurmountable difficulties the early church was victorious. The Gospel message reached to the ends of the earth! It is amazing to note that the same group of men who do not show much promise in the Gospels are the ones functioning so effectively just a few years later in the Book of Acts. In the Gospels we find them quarreling among themselves, wanting positions of authority in the kingdom, jealous of one another and of those outside their group, fleeing when dangers threaten, trying to cast out demons in their own power, and being rather poor examples of future leaders.

Yet under the leadership of this same group of men the whole Roman world and many regions beyond are reached with the Gospel within 70 years. How did they do it? By committing themselves unreservedly to Jesus as Lord and Savior, depending wholeheartedly and solely on the power of the indwelling Holy Spirit, walking with God daily in newness of life, and following Jesus' lifestyle in their ministries. They simply practiced what *he* had taught, modeled, and trained them to do.

We can to with the same effect in our world.

I. THE MINISTRY OF THE HOLY SPIRIT

We have seen how Jesus trained his disciples to carry out God's plan to reach the world. But when will they get the strength to do it? The answer is underscored in Jesus' last words before his ascension:

> *"It is not for you to know the times or dates the Father has set by his own authority. But you will receive power when the Holy Spirit comes on you; and you will be my witnesses in Jerusalem, in all Judea and Samaria, and to the ends of the earth"* (Acts 1:7-8).

These disciples were not to be concerned with the whens and whys of the future; they were simply to carry out the mission assigned to them in the power of the Holy Spirit. Four key expressions may be found in that strategy statement.

1. Power

The Greek word for "power" here is *dunamis*, from which we get the English word "dynamite," speaking of the greatness of the almighty power of God made available to his people for their witnessing. The Good News of Jesus Christ is spiritual dynamite when implanted in the human heart by a witness. When we share our faith with others, we are not doing so in our own abilities, intelligence, experience, or self-determination; we can only be effective witnesses when we trust in the "dynamic" power of the Holy Spirit given to us.

The Holy Spirit gives spiritual dynamite to the human heart through the witness of believers!

The promise here is clear — "you shall receive power." Power is available to us; there can never be a power outage; no storm can tear down the power lines. God's power, the same power that brought all of creation into being and raised the Lord Jesus from the dead, is ours to use in witnessing for Christ.

2. Witnesses

The next expression designates what we are to be. A witness is one who has personally seen, heard, or experienced something and is reporting that action truthfully. We cannot be witnesses to what we have not seen, heard, or experienced. The courts of law call that "hearsay evidence."

The Christian witness must know Christ in a personal relationship, and continue to walk in fellowship with him. We witness to that which is real in our lives.

When we are walking in the Spirit (Gal. 5:16, 26) and filled with the Spirit, then we can be *effective witnesses* for the Lord Jesus Christ.

3. The Progression

The geographical element within the strategy Jesus had and still has for world evangelization is "beginning in Jerusalem, in all Judea and Samaria, and to the ends of the earth." "In Jerusalem" means right where you are — your own neighborhood, city, place of employment, school, and ministry. We are to be witnesses in the power of the Holy Spirit for Christ where we function daily.

"In all Judea" means that we should be concerned for, pray for, and have some witness through our church in the surrounding area beyond our domicile. Some people call this "near neighbor" evangelism, ministering the Gospel of Christ to people similar to us.

"In [all] Samaria" means having a ministry of prayer and witness to others near us of another culture or group. "Unto the ends of the earth" means every tribe, language, people, and ethnic group around the world. It is the responsibility of every Christian to be concerned for and in one way or another have a part in some kind of witness worldwide.

4. The Holy Spirit

Foundational to it all is the ministry of the Holy Spirit. In Acts 1:8, Jesus was reaffirming the promises he gave in the Upper Room Discourse (John 14–16). He stated precisely, "when the Holy Spirit is come upon you." Here is yet another assurance of God's provision for his people. The Holy Spirit will be given to each Christian, and today we know that he has been given — on the Day of Pentecost (Acts 2).

The early disciples, the men and women who gathered with the twelve leaders (Matthias had replaced Judas — Acts 1:15-26), did what Jesus told them to do (Acts 1:7-8). They stayed until they were filled with power. The Spirit affected *in* the early disciples what Christ had done *for* them (John 14:15-21, 25-27; 15:26-27; 16:5-16; 20:21-22). As their indwelling Counselor and Guide, he enabled the disciples and their spiritual successors to carry on the mission of God.

The Book of Acts has sometimes been called "The Acts of the Holy Spirit" because of his prominence in the written record. In nearly every major incident the Spirit is the power behind the scenes. He works powerfully through Peter's sermon on the Day of Pentecost, and the church grows 25 times larger in one day! (Acts 2) The full significance of Pentecost becomes increasingly apparent as the story unfolds. With obvious intent, the growth of the early church is attributed to the Spirit's activity. Over fifty times he is specifically mentioned, more than in any other book of the Bible.

Every believer receives the Holy Spirit (Rom. 8:9). The issue is the submission of the believer to his authority (see Eph. 5:18). We must let the Spirit have his way in our life, and we must do so constantly. "Be filled with the Spirit," (Eph. 5:18) is Paul's admonition. This command is in the plural (meaning it is for all Christians) and in the present tense (it is to be done continuously).

II. THE OBEDIENCE OF THE EARLY CHURCH

The Holy Spirit is given by God to those who obey him (Acts 5:32). Today (particularly in the western world) when it is popular to "do your own thing," the obedience of men and women in the early church stands out as a vibrant testimony to their effectiveness in witnessing for Christ. Discipline of the disciple as he or she follows completely the guidelines in the Bible is vital to the spiritual health of the individual Christian and the church today.

Throughout the Book of Acts, we find loving and willing obedience revealed despite often adverse circumstances. Peter said it best: "We must obey God rather than men!" (Acts 5:29). The whole context of Acts 5:17-42 is an amazing record of obedience by committed disciples in times of grave threat and persecution.

Take the obedience of Stephen as an example (Acts 6:8—7:60). Notice the believers' obedience to proclaim Christ as they were scattered throughout the regions of Judea and Samaria (Acts 8:1-4). Peter's obedience was used to reach a whole Roman household with the gospel (Acts 10:1–11:18).

The obedience of Barnabas and Saul of Tarsus resulted in great growth of an already established church in Antioch of Syria, which ultimately became one of the missionary churches evangelizing the eastern Mediterranean. Subsequently, the obedient leadership sent two of their best people to the "mission field" (Acts 11:19-30; 13:1-3).

In this situation Peter passed to Barnabas Jesus' methodology, who in turn reproduced that training in Saul, soon-to-be Paul. God then used Paul to reproduce the divine plan in the lives of many others. Writing toward the end of his life to his trainee Timothy, Paul said:

> *"You then, my son, be strong in the grace that is in Christ Jesus. And the things you have heard me say in the presence of many witnesses entrust to reliable men who will also be qualified to teach others"* (2 Tim. 2:1-2).

The rest of the Book of Acts shows Paul putting that method of reproduction into practice. In nearly every situation on his three missionary journeys he has a team of people around him into whom he is pouring his life and raising up reliable trainers who are qualified to teach others.

In dependence on the Holy Spirit, the early church brought the good news of Christ's redemption to the very heart of the Roman Empire as Paul and his team arrived in the capital city courtesy of the Roman government (Acts 28:14b-31).

> *"For two whole years Paul stayed [in Rome] in his own rented house and welcomed all who came to see him. Boldly and without hindrance he preached the kingdom of God and taught about the Lord Jesus Christ"* (Acts 28:30-31).

III. FAITHFUL DISCIPLESHIP

The first-century church body existed for ministry. Members of the community shared the servant role of their Lord and, in the way he appointed, continued his mission on earth. That any in the fellowship might be excused from serving does not even seem to cross their minds. All saw themselves as workers together with Christ in reconciling the world to God.

They did this because they were true disciples of the Lord Jesus and were committed to obedience. At the local level elders discipled other Christians in their congregations as did Paul and other missionary team leaders in their mobile ministries. Note the following examples among many:

"And after they had preached the Gospel to that city and had made many disciples, they returned to Lystra and Iconium and Antioch strengthening the souls of the disciples, encouraging them to continue in the faith." (Acts 14:21-22)

"But Paul and Barnabas stayed in Antioch teaching and preaching the word of the Lord with many others also." (Acts 15:35)

"And after some days Paul said to Barnabas, 'Let us return and visit the brethren in every city in which we proclaimed the word of the Lord, and see how they are." (Acts 15:36)

"He [Paul] settled there [Corinth] a year and six months teaching the Word of God among them." *(Acts 18:11)*

Two of the key factors in these effective discipling ministries were:

1) the sense of mission every member had, and

2) the servant example of the leaders (again copying Jesus)

These are expressed beautifully by Paul: "For we do not preach ourselves, but Jesus Christ as Lord, and ourselves as your servants for Jesus' sake" (2 Cor. 4:5).

During this early period, the church flourished in the beauty of holiness. Personal evangelism was practiced naturally because Christians were so in love with Jesus, Christian homes and families were strong, and a variety of societal needs were met by these committed Christians. They were indeed being "salt and light" to their world.

REVIEW BEFORE YOU GO AHEAD

1. Who enables the church to do her ministry?

    _____.

2. Reflect on the background of the early disciples. By society's standards, they were not a very impressive group. Why were these uneducated people able to "turn the world upside down?"

    _____

    _____

    _____

3. How was discipleship practiced in the early church?

    _____.

    _____.

IV. THE UPS AND DOWNS OF CHURCH HISTORY

The history of the church can be written from the perspective of decline and revival. We must learn to copy the successes and avoid the failures.

Spiritual vitality characterized the life of the church for the first few centuries. The witness of God's people impacted the world with power and the church grew mightily. Gradually, however, the fervor of the church faith declined, especially after Christianity was made the official state religion of the Roman Empire under Emperor Constantine (AD 312 ff). Out of a concern for preserving piety and holiness, God raised up the early monastic movement in which committed Christians banded together for mutual strengthening, encouragement, training, and evangelism.

In due course that movement too suffered abuses and became inward-focused; the mission of Christ in evangelism was ignored or forgotten. Periodically there were seasons of refreshing, both inside and outside the official church structure, which served to rekindle the flame of the Spirit in the hearts of God's people. The Reformation (AD 1517 ff) produced a new emphasis on justification by grace through faith, the authority of Scripture, and the priesthood of all believers. In this atmosphere, the principles of discipleship were rediscovered by many in the church. From that time until the present, God has continued to raise up men and women in the church who have sought to obey his Word and minister to others according to his plan.

In times of revival people come alive to God. These awakenings usually are preceded by a *period of stagnation*, when the power of the Church ebbs away. It is a state of spiritual complacency and moral degeneration. Yet as conditions continue to worsen, increasing numbers of Christians develop a *burden of prayer* and seek God's personal intervention.

There comes finally an *hour of decision* when the issues are resolved in judgment or in revival. Ultimately something must give — either sin or the people. It is either repent or perish. Those who repent of their sin and renew their faith will experience renewal.

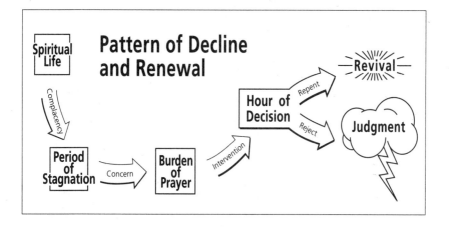

Tragically, however, even among the people who have been blessed, the revival spirit begins to decline. Then the cycle begins all over again with God burdening the hearts of those walking with him to pray for a fresh movement of his Spirit.

But this cycle does not have to be! Through the lives of his faithful, living in consistent communion with him and in the fullness of the Spirit, the fires of revival can be kept aflame in the hearts of those who are discipling or being discipled. If you discern your church has lost sight of its first love, you can set it back on the right track through disciplemaking! The spirit of revival is simply the spirit of normal Christianity, people living in fellowship with God and one another, letting the Holy Spirit have his way in their lives.

♦ The Lessons of History

The lessons of history are plain if we would but see them. Whenever and wherever people follow the biblical principles taught and modeled by Jesus, the church moves forward in the mission of God. Whenever and wherever people forsake the principles, Christians and the church stagnate, and the mission of God is stunted.

If only we would pay attention to the lessons of history! Revival comes when the people of God realize their need, acknowledging that decline has occurred. Convicted of sin, they earnestly pray for mercy. They repent and renew their faith in God. They open the Scriptures to rediscover its principles, and apply them to faith and life. Then, believers begin to live as true disciples of the Lord Jesus Christ, overflowing in love to God, even as they love what God loves — their neighbors as themselves. That is what makes the witness of the church convincing to the world.

REVIEW BEFORE YOU GO AHEAD

1. Which of the following ingredients are usually present in revival movements?

❒ Bible study and prayer   ❒ Highly educated leaders
❒ Conviction of sin   ❒ Renewed burden for evangelism
❒ Organized programs   ❒ Involvement of laity
❒ Obedience   ❒ Political agitation
❒ Social compassion   ❒ Deep concern for holiness

2. Look at the items you have checked. How can those principles be incorporated into the church?

V. THE WORLD SCENE TODAY

In many places the church needs revival today. There is a form of religion but no power — no thrill in personal devotion; no spring in the step; no shout in the soul. The joy of sacrifice is gone. Complacency is the norm.

While the church flounders in mediocrity, the world plunges deeper into sin. For the average person, life has lost its meaning. It is eat, drink and be merry, with everyone for themselves. The sacredness of home and family is forsaken. Standards of decency in public and private are debased. A spirit of lawlessness pervades the land.

But the day of reckoning is coming. Moral and spiritual decline has its limits. There comes a time when we must reap the folly of our ways. Unless something happens soon to change our course, society as we know it is on its way out.

Yet there is hope. Dry bones can live again. In other days when catastrophe has threatened, men and women have turned to God and found in him deliverance and strength. In fact, the greatest spiritual awakenings in the church have come during the darkest times of history. Perhaps the night must close in before we look up and see the stars.

Even now there are some encouraging signs. The multiplication of Bible study and prayer groups, the growing student witness movements, the response to great evangelistic crusades — these, and many other currents of contemporary life point to an awakening concern.

One of the most encouraging signs that God is at work is the renewed emphasis on the discipleship pattern of Jesus. Many churches and para-church ministries as well as individual believers are rediscovering the lifestyle principles of the Great Commission.

This is especially evident in many of the emerging national churches in the so-called Third World countries and the formerly underground churches in nations that had been communist controlled. It is obvious that when biblical principles are followed, the church thrives and grows.

Interestingly, it would seem in our day that the power of the Holy Spirit is most obvious among the "simple," Third World countries, where opportunities for college and seminary training are very limited. Of course, formal education should not be equated with intelligence. Whatever educational advantages we may have, God wants to give revival. An alert mind recognizes the power of God's truth, accepts it without reservation, and begins by faith to live in his promises.

Unfortunately, in much of the developed world today, where materialism abounds, eyes and minds of self-indulging people are easily blinded to the simple reality of God's love and power.

We can rejoice that the Holy Spirit continues his work in the church today, as he has in every age since the Day of Pentecost. And to all who will believe him — truly believe his Word and carry out his mission — the reality of his power is the same as always. Revival will come. The promise holds true:

> *"If my people, who are called by my name, will*
> *humble themselves and pray and seek my face*
> *and turn from their wicked ways, then will I*
> *hear from heaven and will forgive their sin and*
> *will heal their land" (2 Chron 7:14)*

♦ *Ideas to Remember*

This lesson has focused on the use of Jesus' methods by the early church, recorded for us in Scripture in Acts, the Epistles, and Revelation; it has also briefly surveyed the ups and downs of church history, concentrating mainly on the revival and spiritual awakening movements in that 1,900-year period.

We must keep before us the principles studied in Sessions 1 and 2, now seen applied by churches throughout the Christian era. They can be summarized as follows:

- ♦ God has a plan for evangelizing his world.
- ♦ God expects his redeemed people to walk with him in the power of the Spirit.
- ♦ God commands his people to take the Gospel to the ends of the earth beginning where they live.
- ♦ God commands his disciples to reproduce spiritually.
- ♦ God is to get all the glory from the fulfillment of his plan.

These activities of the Holy Trinity — Father, Son, and Holy Spirit — are seen as revelations of the *planner*, the *fulfiller*, and the *facilitator* of God's purposes for his creation.

Application of the Lesson

1. Match the following phrases from Acts 1:7-8 with their implied meaning for our witness:

   "In Jerusalem"   The surrounding area beyond your home

   "In all Judea"   Every tribe, nation, and people group around the world

   "In Samaria"   Right where you are — your own neighborhood

   "The ends of the earth"   Others near you of another culture

   Give examples of how you can be a witness in each of these areas:

   "In Jerusalem": _____

   "In all Judea": _____

   "In Samaria": _____

   "The ends of the earth": _____

2. How would you characterize your life at the present time?
   - ❏ full of the Spirit
   - ❏ cooled off
   - ❏ rather lukewarm
   - ❏ in the deep freeze

3. Get alone with God and make a list of every known sin of which you are aware. Write them down, one by one, until every single thing the Holy Spirit has convicted you of in your life is listed. Confess each sin to God and write I John 1:9 across that sin on the paper. When you finish, destroy the paper.

4. In looking at your life, are you aware of any areas which you have not totally yielded to Christ? If you know of any, surrender them right now.

Prayer of Consecration:

Dear Father,

I confess that there have been things in my life which I have not yielded totally to you. I thank you that you forgive sins and right now I yield every part of my life unreservedly and completely to you. By faith, I claim the fullness of the Holy Spirit in my life.

5. If not already known, memorize Eph. 2:8-9; John 1:12;
    Luke 24:46-48; Acts 1:8 in a Bible version of your choice
    or language.

Mentor Review

Congratulations! You have now completed the
first unit of this course and built a foundation for
what is yet to come in the remaining units. It is time
to meet with your mentor and review with him or her
the biblical principles that are the foundations for
your future follow-up and discipling ministry. Be
sure to *review the scripture memory verses* you
have learned; these verses will assist you greatly in
sharing the Gospel with others.

You should also prayerfully *select someone whom
you can begin to follow-up* in his or her Christian
life. In the coming sessions you will learn many
practical "how-to's"; for now, meet together to share
needs and pray for one another.

You should *review with your mentor the application questions* in this first section. They confront
you and your church with decisions that you must
make on the basis of the biblical data presented in
the three lessons. The decisions you make have the
potential of affecting many lives for Christ in the days
to come.

$\mathcal{U}$NIT TWO:

Establishing
New Believers

SESSION 4
The Process of Follow-up

Introduction to the lesson

Mark and Rachel met in their church high school youth group. Having the usual struggles teenagers do, they managed to "go steady" for a while without getting too intimate and then went to different colleges after graduation. Though they saw each other during vacations when they came home from school and occasionally during the Summers, "the spark" was not there any more. They remained friends and corresponded occasionally, but that was the extent of their relationship.

During the summer between their junior and senior years of college, they both worked at the same summer youth camp in the mountains of Colorado, and gradually their interest in one another came alive again. They had both come to a firm commitment to Jesus Christ as Lord of their lives and had dedicated themselves to his service. As they talked, they discovered that their goals were parallel and the relationship deepened further.

They counseled with some of the staff at the camp, prayed much about their relationship, and became engaged at the end of the Summer. Returning to their respective colleges, they corresponded, called one another frequently, confirmed their God-given love for each other, and made plans for marriage after graduation.

After marriage in their home church in a beautiful Christian wedding, they secured jobs in a nearby city, became involved in a church there, and began ministering to others quite extensively.

Then Rachel became pregnant, eventually gave up her job, and prepared for delivery. Mark took instructions on how to be of help during Rachel's pregnancy, and was an ideal husband during those nine months. Everything went well, and soon the great day arrived.

When the labor pains began, Mark drove Rachel to the hospital and Luke Samuel came into the world. Mark and Rachel congratulated each other on their success. She then packed her things and went home from the hospital leaving the newborn baby behind.

"Well," Mark said contentedly, "we've done our part; the baby is quite healthy and should do well in his life."

"Yes," Rachel replied smiling at the memory, "he's such a nice looking boy, and I'm sure he'll achieve great things for God."

Now this strange ending of an ideal romance, marriage, and birth of a child is completely opposite to anything that a normal mother and father would do in nearly every culture in this world. Many would consider this set of parents as being hard-hearted and uncaring, or ignorant, or stupid, or people who did not want children. It is unthinkable that parents would abandon a helpless infant.

Yet this kind of desertion is happening all over the world many times over each day as new Christians are abandoned by their spiritual parents. Parental care must be given. If you have been blessed being involved in a new convert's commitment, but, for whatever reason, you are unable to devote the "parental care" needed, you should do all you can to see that another discipler assumes this role.

In medicine an obstetrician is concerned with prenatal care and birth, while a pediatrician takes care of the child's formative growth. The terms used for these two practices, then, are *obstetrics* and *pediatrics*. In the spiritual realm *obstetrics* is leading a person to a saving knowledge of Jesus Christ, while *pediatrics* is helping a new Christian grow to spiritual maturity.

But physically the parent plays the most important role. The same is true spiritually. Every new Christian has several needs:

- **Feeding — 1 Peter 2:2**
  "*As newborn babes, desire the pure milk of the Word, that you may grow thereby.*"

- **Protecting — 1 Peter 5:8**
  "*Be sober, be vigilant; because your adversary the devil walks about like a roaring lion, seeking whom he may devour.*"

- **Training — Colossians 2:6,7**
  "*As you have therefore received Christ Jesus the Lord, so walk in Him, rooted and built up in Him and established in the faith, as you have been taught, abounding in it with thanksgiving.*"

Of course, the obstetrician is the one who medically affects the birth. This is the evangelist spiritually. The pediatrician is the one who is trained to care for the new baby in installments. This is the pastor who has the training, experience and common calling to do the same spiritually with a new babe. But, the most important in the final analysis is the parent. This is the one who cares for the new babe on a continual basis. Regardless of how old the child is physically, the older individual who gave birth to the person and nurtured him or her through life is the parent. The truth is analogous spiritually. Spiritual parents are necessary for continued growth in the life of an individual.

Follow-up has been defined as the process of giving continued attention to a new Christian until the person is integrated into the church, discovers her/his place of service, discovers her/his full potential for Jesus Christ, and helps to build Christ's church.

Simply put, follow-up is a process of continual attention which literally means work on a consistent basis with a new believer. This requires *someone*, not just something. Something, of course, is a good Bible study or a guide to the study of the Bible. However, there must be the individual who, as a discipler, gives his or her time to see that the new believer grows in Christ and is maturing in Christ.

By no means should a spiritual *baby* be abandoned from the time of the decision onward. Continual nurturing must be given until the newborn disciple reaches maturity or spiritual "adulthood." This session focuses on guidelines for beginning the process of follow-up or spiritual nurture of new Christians (or older Christians who may never have grown).

Goals for this session

1. You will identify reasons for following-up or establishing new Christians.
2. You will know the process of follow-up and recognize that it is necessary in the local church.
3. You will determine some measurable goals that will set the direction you want to go.
4. You will understand biblical principles running through the whole follow-up process.
5. You will realize what the qualifications are for an effective discipler.

As you begin...

Listen to the messages for Session Four (Cassette Tape 2)

The Lesson

Sensitive evangelists have always been concerned about conserving the fruits of evangelism. All too often in the past, insensitive evangelists and pastors have had many people respond to invitations to receive Christ, but little if any follow-up with those who came forward as inquirers. They assumed those who came to Christ could and would grow on their own. But as in the case of Mark and Rachel's baby, spiritual newborns find it difficult to grow and mature on their own. Both need careful pediatric care. In the spiritual realm, this care or nurturing is called "follow-up," or "establishing." The biblical term and concept of *establishing* is "the ministry of helping a new or immature Christian become grounded in the basics of walking with Christ."

I. SOME REASONS FOR FOLLOW-UP

The usual human response to new instruction is "Why?" This normal question is not a critical response — we want to know the reasons for doing what we have been asked to do. In the Bible God constantly answers the unasked *why* question.

The major reason for follow-up is to *preserve* the new spiritual life of a person who has just come to Christ and to teach him or her how to grow in the Lord. 2 Peter 3:18 says we are to "grow in the grace and knowledge of our Lord and Savior Jesus Christ." Unhappily in the church today we have many *older* Christians who have never grown and probably many more younger or new Christians who never stayed around. Immediate spiritual nurture is necessary for a new Christian, and "older" believers can be helped as well.

> *"They [Paul and Barnabas] returned to Lystra,*
> *Iconium, and Antioch, strengthening the souls of*
> *the disciples, exhorting them to continue in the*
> *faith... Paul said to Barnabas, 'Let us now go*
> *back and visit our brethren in every city where*
> *we have preached the word of the Lord, and see*
> *how they are doing'" (Acts 14:21b-22a; 15:36).*

Another reason for planned follow-up is to give new Christians and older believers the opportunity to experience the joy of growing in their faith and emerge as new church leaders who have been gifted by the Holy Spirit. All of us have seen "late bloomers" who began growing years after they came to Christ. Immediate follow-up would have allowed these men and women to serve in the church years earlier to the glory of God and to the building up of the body.

A third reason is that Jesus demonstrated immediate follow-up as a ministry of his church. He declares in his "Great Commission" statement, "Go and make disciples of all nations…" (Matt. 28:19). He does **not** say, "Go and make converts," but the command is to produce *disciples* by his grace and the power of the Holy Spirit. For converts to grow up in Christ, they must receive careful follow-up. It is a matter of obedience to a clear command of Jesus.

II. THE PROCESS OF FOLLOW-UP

Having discussed the importance of follow-up, we will next examine the process a new believer should follow to grow and mature in the Christian faith. Topics that should be covered in a follow-up relationship include:

- ❏ Helping the new believer receive assurance of salvation.

- ❏ Helping the new believer understand and apply the Word of God.

- ❏ Helping the new believer understand basic Christian doctrine.

- ❏ Helping the new believer understand the basics of the Christian life (e.g. devotional life, prayer, fellowship, etc.).

- ❏ Helping the new believer become a part of a local church.

- ❏ Helping the new believer learn to share Christ with others.

Follow-up involves matching up the new believer with an older, more mature Christian who will become his or her "adoptive parent." This spiritual parent will provide all the ingredients necessary for spiritual growth that parallel the physical growth of a child — love, protection, food, and training. This individualized attention allows the spiritual parent to *tailor-make* the training process according to the unique needs of each new believer.

This was the basic pattern of Jesus' ministry, it was Paul's method

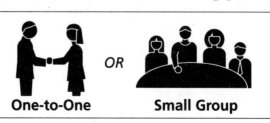

One-to-One   OR   **Small Group**

throughout his ministry, and it is the most effective way for us to fulfill the Great Commission. As in parenting, we spend quality time with another person on an individual basis as well as in a small group. The one-on-one and small group teaching/training formats provide an atmosphere where life-changing learning can take place.

REVIEW BEFORE YOU GO AHEAD

1. Discuss the story of Mark and Rachel. Why do you think that many churches seem not to be sensitive to "spiritual orphans" in their midst?

    _____

    _____

2. Give three reasons why follow-up of new believers is vitally important:

    1) _____

    2) _____

    3) _____

III. OBJECTIVES FOR THE FOLLOW-UP PROCESS

The goal of establishing or follow-up is to see a new or immature Christian become firmly grounded in various aspects of living the Christian life effectively. Paul stated this goal when he said "We proclaim him [Christ], admonishing and teaching everyone with all wisdom, so that we may present everyone perfect [mature] in Christ" (Col. 1:28).

From this goal we can develop a series of objectives that will measure how well we are coming along:

❑   **Doctrinal Objectives** — The new believer should become doctrinally grounded and scripturally oriented. He or she needs to know what the Bible teaches regarding major themes, including such topics as the Bible, God (Father, Son, Holy Spirit), man, sin, salvation, Christian growth and responsibilities, the church, and the last times.

❑ **Devotional Objectives** — The new believer should be introduced to the means of spiritual growth, achieved through a daily devotional time in the Word and prayer. Since the Scriptures are centered on the person of Jesus Christ, our time in them enables us to know him better and become more like him.

❑ **Ministry Objectives** — The new believer should be exposed to a variety of ministry situations to learn by observation and participation. They should learn to share their faith with others. New Christians probably have the largest circle of non-Christian friends and relatives around them than they will ever have the rest of their lives (unless they deliberately set out to cultivate friendships with non-Christians). The new Christian should also learn how to serve others, and, on becoming more mature, be challenged and motivated to become a "multiplier," a spiritual reproducer.

❑ **Character Objectives** — The new believer should begin to develop strong biblical character qualities and work on eliminating negative character traits. This is the essence of the "put on" and "put off" passages in Paul's letters to the Ephesians and to the Colossians (Eph. 4:20-32; Col. 3:5-17). We are to assist younger or non-growing Christians develop their strengths and work on overcoming their weaknesses—as the Bible portrays them.

❑ **Social Objectives** — The new believer should develop a vital family life as well as healthy relationships with other significant persons in the community. A healthy self-esteem enhances their ability to relate gracefully with other people.

IV. BIBLICAL PRINCIPLES IN FOLLOW-UP

Are the above goals and objectives biblical? Are they what God would have us be and do? Let us examine the Word of God for its teaching of these principles.

A. God Wants Every Believer to Grow toward Maturity

Paul states in his letter to the Colossians, "As you have therefore received Christ Jesus the Lord, so walk in him, rooted and built up in him, established in the faith, as you have been taught, abounding in it with thanksgiving" (Col. 2:6-7, NKJV). The three key words reflect growing-to-complete-ness language:

Tree Illustration

Plants your roots on the firm foundation of Jesus Christ to withstand the strong winds of temptation!

1) A tree *roots* into the ground and grows to maturity;
2) A building is *built-up* and is completed;
3) People are *established* and are seen as complete, mature, whole Christians.

Elsewhere Paul notes that it is our responsibility to build on a foundation of salvation in Jesus Christ. But it is our responsibility, hopefully as a "wise master builder," to build on that foundation with the first of two sets of materials — "gold, silver, precious stones" not "hay, wood, straw" (1 Cor. 3:10-17).

B. The Bible Reveals Various Marks of Maturity

In the Scriptures we find some clear and visible marks of a spiritually mature person. Among these are:

1) pursuit of holiness (Heb. 6:1);
2) visible love for others (1 Tim. 1:5);
3) patient endurance in all kinds of situations (1 Cor. 3:13);
4) genuine unity with other Christians (1 Cor. 3:1-3).

C. The Bible Reminds Us that God Is the Source for Spiritual Growth

We are grafted into God's source of strength, sustenance and root system.

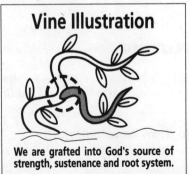

Vine Illustration

We are grafted into God's source of strength, sustenance and root system.

Paul tells the Corinthians that God is the One who causes spiritual growth to occur (1 Cor. 3:6). Jesus taught his disciples in the allegory of the Vine and the Branches, that he as the Vine is the source of growth for the branches (John 15:1-8). The key to that relationship and growth is our "abiding" (having closeness and connection with) in him. That is the only way we can grow to maturity.

Our abiding in Christ means that as a human we are grafted into God's source of strength, sustenance, and his root system. This gives us the ability to minister as necessary in a very needy world and not to be destroyed when the struggles of life are all around us. Of course, Christ does note that abiding in him is a step of faith on the part of the believer. Though we are grafted into Christ at our salvation, the extent to which this graft has occurred and the resulting turn in the life of the believer are a matter of faith on the part of the believer.

D. The Bible Warns of Dangers to Christian Growth

Tragically there are some Christians who start growing, then fall away and grow no more; others never grow after coming to the Savior; yet others fall into sin even in their years of maturity. Jesus himself warns of this danger in his Parable of the Soils (Luke 8:5-15; see also Matt. 13:3-9, 18-23; Mark 4:3-9, 13-20).

This parable teaches that some fall away because of a lack of nourishment in a hostile environment that is not fit for growth. Various trials (testings/temptations) expose the weaknesses that are there and the person has no internal resources to keep growing and gives in to the temptation.

Elsewhere Jesus warns about bad habits that cause people to sin (Matt. 5:28-29) and negative influences of others that lead people astray (Matt. 18:6-14). Paul warns of false doctrines and deceitful spirits that stop young Christians from growing (1 Tim. 4:1). The writer to the Hebrews warns about holding on to an evil and unbelieving heart in a passage where "unbelief" is equated to disobedience (Heb. 3:12-13).

E. Growth Occurs within the Context of Christian Relationships

This is one reason why God has his church, the body of Christ, here on earth, for we grow best within the *vineyard* of other believers. Note all the passages in the New Testament that have to do with one another (for example, Eph. 4:32); these are responsibilities we have toward fellow-believers in mutually assisting one another in spiritual growth. (See such passages as Acts 20:32; 1Peter 2:5; Jude 20.)

This means that the church has a vital role in the establishing of a new Christian and must take seriously its responsibility to assist all its members in their spiritual growth.

F. Spiritual Growth Includes Both Internal and External Aspects

Spiritual growth involves personal growth that is internal [not visible to others] including such disciplines as knowing the Word of God better, building meaningful prayer habits, learning to meditate on Scripture, and adopting Christlike attitudes.

Spiritual growth also includes external activities, such as growth in ministry skills, the visible doing of "good works" (see Eph. 2:10), growing improvement in relationships, and sharing one's faith without embarrassment and at every opportunity.

G. Spiritual Growth Is a Lifelong Process

The persistent call of Scripture is for all of us to be lifelong learners; we never in this life arrive at absolute perfection until we reach heaven. Thus all of us — older and younger Christians — must learn that the call to discipleship is ours from God all the days of our lives. It is such a thrill to hear an 80-year-old saint of God say: "Let me share with you what God taught me this past week and what I learned of him in the Word!"

There are many examples of this attitude in Scripture. Caleb was still growing and going at the age of 85. "Give me this mountain!" he cried, then he assumed the most difficult military task in the Land of Canaan because "he *wholly* followed the Lord his God!" (Josh. 14:12a, 14).

Overview of Disciplemaking Ministry

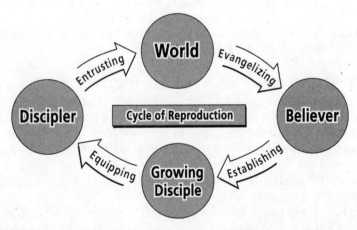

H. Spiritual Growth Includes the Whole Person

Human beings are not disjointed or divided; when God created us in his own image, he made us *whole* people. We dare not divide ourselves into soul and body, as though one part of us does one thing and the other does something else. The language of Scripture that says, "Love the Lord your God with all your heart and with all your soul and with all your strength" (Deut. 6:5) is a Hebrew way of saying, "Love God totally with everything that you are and have!"

Paul emphasizes this when he gives his closing benediction in one of his letters: "May God himself, the God of peace, sanctify you through and through. May your whole spirit, soul and body be kept blameless at the coming of our Lord Jesus Christ" (1 Thess. 5:23).

V. QUALIFICATIONS OF A DISCIPLER

It is necessary at this point to note the qualifications of a person who would follow up a younger Christian. Since much of the ministry involves being an example, the Bible sets forth some standards and qualifications for a person discipling another.

Obviously, you must be *surrendered to the Lordship of Christ*. Without this commitment you do not have the foundation to be an example to a younger believer.

A discipler must also have a *love and concern for people*. Discipling is a ministry that costs in terms of time and personal exposure. Those who would give their lives in service for others must have this spirit of love and compassion.

Another crucial characteristic is *holiness*. This does not mean that you must be perfect, but your life should be characterized by a zealous pursuit of holiness (Heb. 12:14). You should avoid being involved in anything that will cause weaker Christians to stumble.

You must be *open and transparent*. Discipleship is a costly ministry in terms of exposure. New believers will see not only your strengths but also your weaknesses and inconsistencies.

A discipler must be a *pace-setter* in key disciplines of the Christian life. The new Christian must not only hear you talk about your devotional life, prayer life, and witnessing, he or she should see evidence of it on a regular basis. You must be practicing what you are teaching to others. The Apostle Paul could say, "The things you have *learned* and *received* and *heard* and *seen* in me, practice these things..." (Phil. 4:9).

Many other important characteristics could be cited, but one must be highlighted. You must **understand what your role is** in the process and what God's role is. In 1 Cor. 3:6, the Apostle Paul says, "I planted, Apollos watered, but God gives the growth." God alone can bring growth in a person's life. The discipler is a catalyst for that growth, but you should never allow yourself to believe that you are bringing it about.

This kind of person will effectively help another Christian grow. The main point is this: it takes a disciple to make a disciple. You cannot challenge someone else to grow unless you are growing and maturing yourself. But on the other hand it is vital to realize that you don't need to be "miles" down the road spiritually before you can help someone else! You only need to be steady on your feet to help someone else begin to walk!

♦   *Ideas to Remember*

The whole concept of following up new Christians can be described as spiritual pediatrics; that is, the care and nurture given to spiritual babies. When a person is born again, he or she is spiritually like a newborn baby and needs all the care that a parent would give that child. All too often Christians and churches have not taken care of the newborn in their midst. The call of Scripture is for believers and their assemblies to take care of the spiritual newborn among them.

The biblical term for this ministry is *establishing* a person in his or her faith. This session focused on the following:

- ❐   Three reasons why immediate follow-up is a vital necessity.

- ❐   The process of follow-up is the personal attention given to a new Christian.

- ❐   The goals of follow-up are to see the new Christian gain assurance, become mature in his or her faith and become a spiritual reproducer.

- ❐   Follow-up has doctrinal objectives, devotional objectives, ministry objectives, character-building objectives, and social objectives.

- ❐   Eight biblical principles for this ministry were discussed in the last section.

KEY: We as Christians must have commitment as individuals and as churches to a deliberately planned ministry of follow-up.

Application of the Lesson

Here are some questions for reflection and application:

1. Think about your own Christian experience. Did anyone (e.g. parent, Sunday School teacher, friend) help you learn to walk with God in your early days as a believer? If so, what did that person do that was so helpful?

2. If no one helped you grow spiritually, how did you come to the place that you did indeed start growing?

3. Check how you have helped someone else to grow in his or her spiritual life.
    - ❏ frequent calls
    - ❏ visited regularly
    - ❏ get together for prayer
    - ❏ study Bible together
    - ❏ go to church together
    - ❏ take vacation together
    - ❏ personal letters/cards
    - ❏ taken places with you
    - ❏ work together
    - ❏ encouragement
    - ❏ counsel
    - ❏ ask their advice/help

4. What commitment do you need to make to begin or continue the ministry of follow-up in and through your church?

5. If you are not yet working with a new or stagnant Christian to help him or her grow spiritually, continue to pray that God would bring someone into your life whom you can follow-up. Write down one or two names of people you think would be a possibility and pray for God's direction in the relationship.

    1) _____ 2)_____

6. Memorize John 5:24; Rom. 10:9-10 and Col. 1:28; 2:6-7 in a Bible version of your choice.

SESSION 5
Following up a New Believer

Introduction to the Lesson

In his book *The Holy Spirit*, Billy Graham states the following as vital to the biblical process of establishing new believers in their faith (page 147):

> *One of the first verses of Scripture that Dawson Trotman, founder of The Navigators, made me memorize was, "The things that thou hast heard of me among many witnesses, the same commit thou to faithful men, who shall be able to teach others also" (2 Tim. 2:2 KJV). This is a little like a mathematical formula for spreading the gospel and enlarging the Church. Paul taught Timothy; Timothy shared what he knew with faithful men; these faithful men would then teach others also. And so the process goes on and on. If every believer followed this pattern, the Church would reach the entire world with the gospel in one generation! Mass crusades, in which I believe and to which I have committed my life, will never finish the Great Commission; but a one-by-one ministry will.*

Pastors and church leaders must catch the vision for this ministry and train the members of their congregations to help younger Christians grow. These new believers, as they grow to maturity, will in turn know how to help the next generation of younger Christians grow in their faith, thus continuing the cycle.

Gene Warr, a Christian businessman, has been active in this kind of ministry for many years. He tells the story of ministering to a younger man named Paul, spending two hours with him monthly, investing life and experience. He helped him with some of his problems, some weak areas of his ministry, and speaking in public. After a while Paul began meeting with a fellow student named Bob and reproducing in his life what Gene had taught him.

Some time later Bob led a pair of twins, Rick and Bob, to Christ, then began to invest his life in theirs. They in turn led others to

Christ, followed them up, and discipled them to reproduce. So Gene concludes with a flow chart of those who ministered to others (*Making Disciples,* pages 49-50):

As Gene had been helped by Charlie Riggs, who had been followed up and trained by Lorne Sanny, so he in turn reproduced what he had learned to many generations. When that kind of string is reproduced a hundred or a thousand times, the goal of reaching the world with the Gospel becomes a real possibility in our generation.

> Dawson Trotman
> ➡ Lorne Sanny
> ➡ Charlie Riggs
> ➡ **Gene Warr**
> ➡ Paul
> ➡ Bob
> ➡ Rick and Bob
> ➡ Many Others

Goals for this session

1. You will understand what is necessary for the spiritual growth of new believers.

2. You will know how to give immediate care to a person just converted.

3. You will be able to help one come to an assurance of salvation.

4. You will know how to encourage new believers during the first few weeks of their new life in Christ, motivating them to have a quiet time, learn how to pray, memorize Scripture, and take sermon notes.

5. You will see the importance of the local church for a new believer's spiritual growth.

As you begin...

Listen to the messages for Session Five (Cassette Tape 2)

The Lesson

The whole process of spiritual growth begins with basic teachings which the Apostle Peter calls "the pure milk of the word" (NKJV) — basic Christian truths that the new believer needs to know. The NIV expresses this challenge by Peter in this way: "Like newborn babies, crave pure spiritual milk, so that by it you may grow up in your salvation" (1 Peter 2:2).

This "spiritual milk" will include some of the following basic teachings and experiences needed by a new believer to start spiritual growth:

- ❑ **Assurance of salvation** — what the Bible says about what has happened in his or her life.

- ❑ **Christian fellowship** — time with a discipler and becoming part of a local assembly of fellow-believers.

- ❑ **Beginning disciplines** — learning how to walk with God through the Word and prayer, both individually and in concert with others.

- ❑ **Evangelistic motivation** — sharing what God has done in his or her life with others.

- ❑ **Prayer** — knowing that access to God is available and practicing talking with him.

I. PRACTICAL GUIDELINES FOR THIS MINISTRY

How do we begin? Start by noting some practical guidelines for implementing follow-up with a new Christian. We must realize and be sensitive to the fact that the first week of a new believer's life in Christ is crucial to ongoing spiritual growth. If a new convert is followed up immediately, growth can begin and the person can move forward in his or her Christian life; if follow-up does not occur, he or she will oftentimes drift, remain a spiritual baby, and could easily fall away.

Follow-up is initially the building of a relationship. It is not just the passing on of material from one notebook to another; it is a shared life experience. It must be ***person-centered,*** not materials-centered (although biblically based materials can serve an important purpose). We must know well those whom we are helping, for people grow spiritually at different rates, come from a variety of situations in life, and have different personal needs. People also have different personalities and will respond to help differently.

One thing to remember in a follow-up relationship is that there should be both structured and unstructured time together. Structured time is when we meet for instruction and accountability; unstructured time is when we get to know one another in the normal course of doing things together (bowling, going to a concert, football game, quilting, and other activities).

When working with another person, be sure to commend and encourage the trainee when he or she learns something new. A good pattern would be 90% encouragement and 10% correction (gently and lovingly done). We must realize that in any follow-up situation various problems might arise, and some of these may require professional help — pastor, counselor, psychologist. Be a good listener, a great encourager, and a consistent example.

As a necessary safeguard, work only with persons of the same gender. Serious problems may arise if we try to follow-up persons of the opposite sex. Stable couples, however, can work well with other couples who might have come to Christ together.

Be sure that the Scriptures are the chief source of the teaching of principles, not what "I think" or what "my church says." It is always safest to be on the ground of "This is what the Word of God teaches!"

While it is God who brings growth in people's lives, he uses people as part of the process. What a privilege to be the instrument that God uses to encourage growth in another!

II. CLOSE INVOLVEMENT WITH ANOTHER PERSON

The ministry of follow-up involves closeness. We will be getting to know each other better, spending quality time together, and growing together in the Lord.

Like most ministries that put action to the Word, the key to this ministry is prayer. Observe how often the Apostle Paul mentions that he is praying for new believers (e.g. Phil. 1; Col. 1; I Thess. 1:2; Gal. 4:19). Paul understood that the Christian life is not a playground, but a battleground. Prayer is the weapon of spiritual warfare.

The discipler must meet with the new believer as quickly as possible after conversion (preferably within 24 — 48 hours). In the initial meeting most of the following ingredients should occur:

- ☐ Express a sincere interest in the person's life.

- ☐ Clarify and confirm his\her commitment to Christ. Ask the person to express thanksgiving to God for salvation. If the person hesitates, find out why. Praise is natural to a child of God.

- ☐ Explain the new personal relationship a believer now has with Jesus Christ.

- ☐ Note the importance of identifying with a local church.

- ☐ Briefly instruct in the basic disciplines of the Christian life:

- ☑ Reading the Bible daily
- ☑ Studying the Bible regularly
- ☑ Memorizing Scripture
- ☑ Praying consistently and intelligently
- ☑ Sharing Christ with relatives and friends
- ☑ Learning to obey what God says to do

Exchange phone numbers and addresses; make yourself available to the new Christian at any time; make arrangements to get together within the next week; and get other Christians to contact this person informally so that he or she will come to know other believers.

The prime qualities for growth that we must transmit immediately to a new believer are a deep desire for fellowship with Jesus Christ and consistency. The former includes introducing a daily Bible reading and prayer lifestyle, while the latter involves the example of the discipler together with small, doable assignments, much encouragement, and low-key checkup.

REVIEW BEFORE YOU GO AHEAD

1. What is meant by "person-centered" versus "materials-centered?"

_____

_____

2. What was cited as the key to the ministry of follow-up?

_____

III. ASSURANCE OF SALVATION

The first teaching and affirmation a new Christian needs is assurance of salvation. The major reason for this is that Satan will attack a new believer with doubts in this area of his or her fresh experience in Christ. Satan's tactic after he has lost a person to the Lord is to deceive the new believer into thinking that his decision or commitment was not real and that God will not fulfill his promises to him. To counter these attacks the new believer must have assurance of salvation *from Scripture*.

"And this is the testimony: God has given us eternal life, and this life is in his Son. He who has the Son has life; he who does not have the Son of God does not have life. I write these things to you who believe in the name of the Son of God so that you *may know* that you have eternal life" (1 John 5:11-13).

Discuss with your trainee what God has said. If the new believer has asked Jesus to come into his life, he has life. His grounding for this assurance must be in Scripture. Ask him/her, "Have you trusted God for your salvation?"

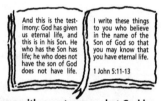

And this is the testimony: God has given us eternal life, and this is in his Son. He who has the Son has life; he who does not have the son of God does not have life.

I write these things to you who believe in the name of the Son of God so that you may know that you have eternal life.

1 John 5:11-13

Discuss with your trainee what God has said.

If the person whom you are following up still seems to have doubts about salvation, perhaps there had never been a true commitment to begin with. This means that you will have to lead the individual through a Gospel presentation and invite the person to receive Christ. Use any presentation with which you are comfortable; the one that will be suggested in this course is one version of the Bridge Illustration (also found in the tract by Billy Graham, *Steps to Peace with God*; [you are presently memorizing the Bible verses for this presentation]). Another helpful tool produced by the Billy Graham Evangelistic Association is a series of three booklets: *Knowing God, Following Christ*, and *Sharing Christ* (See Appendix C).

If you are still uncertain about the person's salvation after the answers, go through your presentation of the Gospel, ask, "Is there any good reason *why* you cannot pray to receive Christ as your Lord and Savior while we are here together?" If the person is ready, lead the individual through a commitment prayer; if the person is not prepared to do so at that time, continue the relationship with the prayer that the person will do so soon.

In your conversation you will need to explore the person's initial feelings, what some doubts might be, or what questions the individual may have about the Christian life. Remember, some of the new Christians may come out of a totally non-Christian and secular background.

Other Scriptures you may want to study with your new trainee are:

♦ *John 5:24* .... (emphasis on the assurance of those who believe in Jesus)

♦ *Philippians 1:6* .... (Jesus' promise to continue working in us)

♦ *Matthew 7:24-27* ..... (the contrast between building our lives on God's Word or feelings only)

♦ *1 John 5:1-3* .... (emphasis again on the Word of God bringing us assurance)

♦ *Romans 8:1* .... (God's categorical statement that those who are in Christ no longer are under condemnation).

IV. FIRST STEPS OF GROWTH

After helping the new believer build assurance based on the Word of God, begin introducing the Bible's teaching on what constitutes spiritual growth. This is what the Bible calls a walk with God [Christ]. We walk with him by taking in the Word of God by every means available to us, and we converse with him through prayer.

Before you begin the time of instruction, however, you will need to explain to your trainee what a mentoring relationship is all about and what its purpose is. Clarify how God has given Christians to one another for the purpose of helping each other to grow spiritually. As someone else has helped me grow, I now want to help another Christian grow as well (see Matt. 10:8). Whatever growth materials you might use, explain their purpose and how you will be using them *together*. Then set a time to meet weekly (if possible), making the meetings (time and place) convenient for the new Christian's time and schedule, usually 1 to 1½ hours per meeting.

A. The Daily Quiet Time

In order for your trainee to receive the necessary spiritual nourishment for growth, a daily time with the Lord through the

Word and prayer is important. This has been called "the quiet time," a time we set apart each day to meet with God (see Psalm 46:10a).
> *"God is faithful, through whom you were called into fellowship with his Son, Jesus Christ our Lord" (1 Cor. 1:9, NASB).*

Why should a new Christian have a Quiet Time? Jesus displayed an example for us to follow in Mark 1:35 when he spent time with the Father in the early morning (cf. Luke 5:15-16). Others who have been persons of God have set aside time to fellowship with him: Abraham (Gen. 19:27); Jacob (Gen. 28:18); Moses (Exod. 34:2); David (Psalm 5:3); and Daniel (Dan. 6:10). Their example sets a clear pattern for us to follow.

We also obtain wisdom and strength for facing life's trials and temptations by spending time with the Lord (Matt. 4:4b; James 1:2-4). We obtain guidance for difficult decisions by spending time in God's Word and in prayer (Psalm 119:105; Prov. 3:5-6; Psalm 143:8).

The Billy Graham Evangelistic Association recommends that a new Christian start with a fifteen-minute daily quiet time:

Daily Quiet Time
5 minutes .... **Time of Prayer:** Adoration, Confession, Thanksgiving, Intercession, Petition.
5 minutes .... **Reading the Bible:** A pre-planned short passage.
5 minutes .... **Application:** What does the passage tell you about daily living?

As the new disciple grows, doubtless the time given to prayer will grow. (See Appendix A for more information on having a daily Quiet Time).

Illustration

These principles can be illustrated by the use of human hands, one which we will call The Prayer Hand (left), the other The Word Hand (right). The fingers on each of the hands illustrate the five kinds of prayer found in the Bible and the five ways of taking in God's Word. You can use your own hands to indicate the points (see next page for illustration).

The fingers of the Prayer Hand, beginning with the pointing finger, moving to the little finger, then the thumb, indicate the following:

- ◆ Prayers of adoration .... praising God for who he is (pointing finger)

- ◆ Prayers of confession .... agreeing with God about my sin (middle finger)

- ◆ Prayers of intercession .... praying for the needs of others (ring finger)

- ◆ Prayers of petition .... praying for my own needs (little finger)

- ◆ Prayers of thanksgiving ... praising God for what he has done and is doing for me and others (thumb)

All of the above are prayers which we pray *by faith,* believing that God will answer them according to his will and to his glory.

The fingers of the Word Hand, beginning with the little finger and moving toward the thumb, indicate the following:

- ◆ Hearing God's Word for *faith*

- ◆ Reading God's Word for *fellowship*

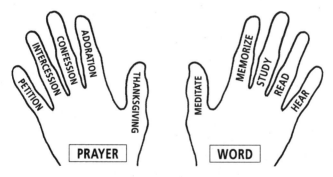

The Hands Illustration

- ◆ Studying God's Word for *knowledge*

- ◆ Memorizing God's Word for *effectiveness*

- ◆ Meditating on God's Word for *understanding*

We then apply God's Word appropriated by the above five means for *continued growth.*

B. Scripture Memory

Another discipline the new believer should be encouraged to begin is to memorize the Word of God. This valuable exercise is one of the greatest resources we have to live effectively as growing Christians. The psalmist wrote, "I have hidden your word in my heart that I might not sin against you" (Psalm 119:11). One believer testifies to the significance of Scripture Memory in his life:

> When I first became a Christian while in the U. S.
> Navy, I had many doubts and struggles because
> there was no one around to help me grow. Then
> I met a fellow-believer who, when he heard my
> sad story, pulled out a little packet from his
> pocket called *Initial B[ible]-Rations* and said,
> "Memorize two of these verses each week and I
> will check you out on them." I did, and they with
> many others since then have served me well
> these 38 years. These four verses were: Assur-
> ance of Salvation—1 John 5:11-12; Assurance of
> Victory—1 Corinthians 10:13; Assurance of For-
> giveness—1 John 1:9; and Assurance of Provi-
> sion—John 16:24.

How does Scripture memory help you? It...

(1) helps you resist *temptation* (Psalm 119:9-11)

(2) directs your thoughts towards the things of God (Phil. 4:8).

(3) provides help when you *need it most*. You will not always have a Bible with you, but you can always carry with you the verses you have memorized.

(4) equips you to *share Christ* with others.

(5) gives you direction for daily *decisions*.

Many Scripture memory plans are available today in Christian bookstores. You can follow one of these plans or simply choose verses yourself to memorize. The important thing is to hide God's Word in your heart! (See Appendix B for more information on memorizing Scripture).

C. Sermon Notetaking

One of the main reasons for going to a church is to have a steady diet of good biblical preaching — hearing the Word of God for the purpose of building and strengthening faith. At this point you might instruct your trainee to take effective sermon notes to retain the lessons God is teaching him/her weekly through the pastor. The miracle of preaching is that God can use one sermon to meet the needs of many people in one congregation. Notes should be taken on what specifically speaks to the individual hearer (not necessarily reproducing the pastor's beautiful three-point outline).

Notetaking helps you...
(1) *listen* more intently;
(2) make *personal applications;*
(3) *retain* the message;
(4) be able to *share* it with others.

Notetaking Aids Learning

V. ASSOCIATING WITH A LOCAL CHURCH

New converts need to meet together with other believers in a nearby church that teaches and preaches the Word of God. Here is where the new Christian will grow along with others. The new believer should also witness to his/her faith by baptism, a point of open identification with Christ and his death and resurrection.

The church, imperfect as it is, has been brought into being by God Himself so that its members, redeemed men and women, might (1) gather together to worship the Lord, (2) strengthen one another, and (3) witness to the world. Disciples of the Lord Jesus Christ need to associate themselves with a local church so that they can carry out the God-given mandate in the above three areas.

A. We Are to Worship Almighty God

True worship is real Christians gathering together in a given locality to give to the Lord the praise and thanksgiving he deserves. Each disciple's responsibility is to worship God in concert with other believers and to do so regularly (Heb. 10:25) in spirit and truth (John 4:24). It is a spiritual activity that comes from a sincere heart and is given lovingly and willingly to our Lord and Savior.

We can certainly worship God alone in the solitude of our daily quiet time, but the call of Scripture is for all of God's people to gather regularly for corporate worship as well (Heb. 10:24-25). In the Old

Testament Israel worshipped on the Sabbath, the seventh day; since the resurrection of Jesus the New Testament church worshipped him on the first day of the week, our Sunday.

B. We Are to Build up Fellow Believers

A second responsibility Jesus' disciples have corporately is to build up fellow Christians within the church. This is to be done individually ("each other," one-on-one) and in groups of varying sizes ("one another," one-to-others). In addition to taking sermon notes, we should be part of a group learning the Scriptures (Sunday school, adult education, mid-week Bible study). Later we may lead a group in study or teach a class.

C. We Are to Be Witnesses to the World

The third corporate responsibility of Christian disciples is to present to the world a united visible picture of love in action. Jesus stated on the evening before he went to the cross, "A new commandment I give to you, that you love one another; as I have loved you, that you also love one another. *By this all will know that you are my disciples,* if you have love for one another" (John 13:34-35, italics added). It is the corporate witness of Christian men and women loving one another that serves as a powerful testimony of the reality of God and his salvation in this world.

Training for evangelism and opportunities for neighborhood calling are ideally to be found in the local church. This is why a disciple must associate with a group of men and women committed to that responsibility in a given location. If the new believer can be shown that witness and sharing one's faith is a *natural* outcome of being a Christian, starting immediately, the new Christian will be a witness for life. (Details on sharing our faith and presenting the Gospel in a number of effective ways will be discussed in detail in Lesson 8.)

♦ Ideas to remember

The whole teaching on beginning follow-up may be summarized in the following two segments:

The new Christian needs to know:
- ☑ Assurance of salvation

- ☑ Basic Christian doctrines

The new Christian needs to begin these disciplines (which are basic, yet do not take too much time):

☑ Having a daily quiet time

☑ Learning to pray

☑ Memorizing Scripture

☑ Sermon Notetaking

☑ Becoming involved in a local church

☑ Sharing the faith with relatives and friends

In beginning follow-up make sure that the new believer has assurance of salvation, that the person knows that he/she is indeed born again (see 1 John 5:13). On this foundation, then, the other Christian disciplines can be built.

Application of the Lesson

Here are some questions for reflection and application.

1. As a teacher, how can you insure the new Christian understands the basis for the assurance of eternal salvation?

2. List three reasons for the new convert's need to associate with a local church.

    (1) _____

    (2) _____

    (3) _____

3. Draw a picture of the Word Hand and the Prayer Hand as they currently look in your own life. Indicate by the length of the fingers which areas need attention.

4. What were the main ideas you got from the last sermon you heard?

5. Memorize 1 John 5:11-13; John 16:24; 1 Cor. 10:13; and 1 John 1:9 in a Bible version of your choice.

S ESSION 6
Discipling a New Believer

Introduction to the Lesson

A fascinating memorandum has been making its rounds in Christian circles. Whether "discovered" in some archaeological dig or "found" in some ancient records, it applies well to the topic of discipleship.

From: Jordan Management Consultants
To: Jesus, Son of Joseph,
Woodcrafters Carpenter Shop,
Nazareth, Galilee 25922

Dear Sir:

Thank you for submitting the resumes of the twelve men you have picked for management positions in your new organization. All of them have taken our battery of tests; and we have not only run the results through our computer, but also arranged personal interviews for each of them with our psychologist and vocational aptitude consultant.

The profiles of all tests are included and you will want to study each of them carefully. As part of our service and for your guidance, we make some general comments, much as an auditor will include some general statements. This is given as a result of staff consultation and comes without any additional fee.

It is the staff opinion that most of your nominees are lacking in background, education, and vocational aptitude for the type of enterprise you are undertaking. They do not have the team concept. We would recommend that you continue your search for persons of experience in managerial ability and proven capability.

Simon Peter is emotionally unstable and given to fits of temper. Andrew has absolutely no qualities of leadership. The two brothers, James and John, the sons of Zebedee, place personal interest above company loyalty. Thomas demonstrates a questioning attitude that would tend to undermine morale. We feel that it is our duty to tell you that Matthew has been blacklisted by the Greater Jerusalem Better Business Bureau. James, the son of Alphaeus, and Thaddeus definitely have radical leanings, and they both registered a high score on the manic depressive scale.

One of the candidates, however, shows great potential. He is a man of ability and resourcefulness, meets people well, has a keen business mind, and has contacts in high places. He is highly motivated, ambitious, and responsible. We recommend Judas Iscariot as your controller and right hand man. All of the other profiles are self-explanatory.

We wish you every success in your new venture.

Sincerely yours,
Jordan Management Consultants

What the "Jordan Management Consultants" missed completely was the grace of God that overcomes human weaknesses and makes out of "failures" great men of God. It is the Lord Jesus Christ who takes weak human vessels and makes great spiritual leaders of history.

The writer to the Hebrews gives us a glimpse into the heroes of the faith in the Old Testament (Hebrews 11), while the records of church history portray the many changed men and women who affected their generations with the Gospel of Jesus Christ. Space does not allow even the mention of a few of these, but the crucial point that both Scripture and history make is that most of these had a mentor who helped them grow in Christ.

Today we call that *discipleship*, and helping another Christian become a worker in the harvest fields of the world is called the process of *discipling*. A *disciple*, then, can be defined as a committed follower of Jesus Christ, one who is willing to be a lifelong learner of the Lord. *Discipleship* is the process of living as a disciple, and *discipling* is helping another Christian become a disciple in the full meaning of that term scripturally, then continue in that commitment, and reproduce it in the life of another.

Thus the next stage of establishing a new believer is to *disciple* him or her in the Christian life and ministry.

Goals for this session

1. You will be able to see the whole picture of what is involved in ongoing follow-up or establishing.

2. You will introduce personal Bible study and meditation as another discipline to follow in this stage.

3. You will learn to teach an effective Gospel presentation to your trainees.

As you begin...

Listen to the messages for Session Six (Cassette Tapes 2-3)

The Lesson

I. SEEING THE WHOLE PICTURE

In order to be effective in our discipling ministries we must see the whole picture of what is involved in this stage of the establishing or follow-up process. That's what the Apostle Paul did in his ministry: "Then they returned to Lystra, Iconium, and Antioch, strengthening the disciples and encouraging them to remain true to the faith" (Acts 14:21b-22a).

Ongoing follow-up is based on the new believer's willingness to make some additional commitments for spiritual growth. One of these commitments is to become more consistent in all of the Christian disciplines and activities; another is to learn to do personal Bible study.

There are other activities. The growing disciple must become more involved in the learning and ministry opportunities of his or her local church, more consistent in witness to Jesus Christ, and more active in outreach through the church.

Although people grow at different rates and have different needs, there are certain truths about the Christian faith and growth that are foundational and need to be dealt with early in the Christian life. Some of these may be demonstrated in an illustration developed by Dawson Trotman, founder of The Navigators.

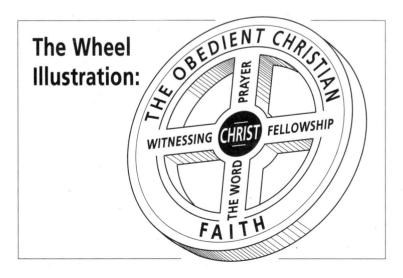

The Wheel Illustration:

The concept of a wheel is known in virtually every culture in the world. *The Wheel Illustration* demonstrates vividly the truth that Jesus Christ must be at the center and focus around which our lives revolve even as the hub is the center of the wheel (2 Cor. 5:17; John 15:5; Gal. 2:20); the rim is where the wheel touches the road and is also visible to all, picturing for us the obedient Christian living the Spirit-filled life by faith (Heb. 11:6). The spokes on a turning wheel are invisible, but vitally necessary to get power from the hub to the rim. They must be balanced for the wheel to roll smoothly.

The spiritual "spokes" are The Word of God, Prayer, Fellowship, and Witness; the first two having to do with our vertical relationship (with God), the second two having to do with our horizontal relationships (with people) — fellowship with Christians and a witness given to unbelievers. Faith, the tire, absorbs the impact of life and bounces back as a tire under air pressure rebounds from the obstacles in travel. The illustration admirably pictures what a disciple's life ought to look like.

To this general illustration we would attach specific training objectives for this stage of ongoing follow-up. These would be:

♦ Continued strengthening of already begun disciplines—the quiet time, prayer, Scripture memory, and sermon note-taking.

♦ Beginning the disciplines of personal Bible study and meditation on Scripture.

♦ Learning a Gospel presentation and having greater involvement in evangelistic outreach.

♦ Becoming involved in the life and ministry of a local church.

♦ Starting to work on some specific character development to become more like Jesus Christ.

♦ Knowing what the whole process of establishing involves in order to become convinced of the process of spiritual reproduction.

Draw your wheel at this time with the length of the spokes accurately showing the balance that you feel your life is in presently.

II. CONTINUING DISCIPLINES

In the first stage of follow-up we began some foundational disciplines with the new believer. The new Christian was challenged to begin a quiet time, using the Bible and learning how to pray, and hopefully was motivated to start memorizing Scripture to resist doubts and temptations. It was suggested that the new believer share what had happened in his/her life with relatives and friends. The individual was asked to take some sermon notes while listening to messages.

These were given more as suggestions than requirements, more of a *helping* method than a *teaching-training* method. Now is the time to begin serious teaching-training. From now on the teaching and training will be more structured, will include more materials, and will take more time, both in the meeting and in preparation. The accountability part of each session will involve sharing of quiet time insights from the previous week, reciting of Scripture memory verses from previous weeks, discussing sermon notes, and times of prayer. Both discipler and trainee will be working on having these disciplines become more consistent in their respective lives.

REVIEW BEFORE YOU GO AHEAD

1. Discuss the implications of the "Jordan Management Consultants" memo for your own personal ministry.

   _____

   _____

   _____

   _____

2. Summarize the Wheel Illustration in your own words.

   _____

   _____

   _____

   _____

   _____

3. Which three specific training objectives seem most relevant to you at present? To your disciple?

   _____

   _____

   _____

   _____

III. BIBLE STUDY AND MEDITATION

In this stage of ongoing follow-up or discipling you will take up two additional disciplines not suggested thus far. They will be two more ways in which we can take in the Word of God, and will require more effort and time than the previous three.

Personal Bible study is digging into the Scriptures to gain knowledge of the Word of God. We find a wide variety of studies available today. The main ingredient of this discipline is personal application, as the student of the Word of God puts into practice what the person is getting from the Scripture.

For a new Christian, begin with a simple study that is in the question-and-answer format. Simple questions are asked, a Bible reference is given, the student then answers the question in his or her own words. Every so often an application question is asked, so that the truths being learned might be applied to life. Excellent studies of this type are available from the Billy Graham Evangelistic Association, Campus Crusade for Christ, the Navigators, InterVarsity, Christian Outreach, etc.

Many additional studies are available from both denominational and interdenominational publishers. Choose the one that will be most effective in the new believer's life as you perceive it.

As Christians grow, they should learn to study the Bible on their own. A simple format for personal Bible Study can follow these three questions:

1) *What does this passage say?* — *Discovery*

2) *What does it mean?* — *Understanding*

3) *How does it relate to me?* — *Application*

In addition your trainee needs to begin *meditating on the Word of God.* Meditation is not the emptying of the mind, but *thinking deeply* about God's truths. This discipline is a very valuable spiritual exercise, for we can learn so much of God's Word through it, as well as growing in our faith and understanding. When we give *attention* to God's word through meditation, his intention is to change our lives, for God's word never returns without a spiritual profit. (Isah. 55:10)

IV. LEARNING A GOSPEL PRESENTATION

Many excellent Gospel presentations are available an being used effectively today, such as the Evangelism Explosion approach of D. James Kennedy and his team, the "Four Spiritual Laws," developed by Bill Bright and the Campus Crusade for Christ, and various forms of the Bridge Illustration and Billy Graham's "Steps to Peace with God." Each of these approaches includes the basic biblical teaching on what is included in a Gospel presentation. Although verse references may vary slightly, the essential ingredients of a Gospel presentation with related Bible passages are:

♦ What persons are apart from God — sinners (Rom. 3:23 and others)

♦ What God has done for people — salvation through Christ (Rom. 5:8 and others)

♦ How persons can receive that salvation and enter into a relationship with Jesus Christ (John 1:12 and others)

As a first step, the witness focuses on the listener's current state of separation from God, in effect establishing a felt need. A felt need is a motivation in an individual to seek fulfillment of a personalized desire. In this case, that desire is reconciliation with God. The only exception to Romans 3:23 is Jesus Christ himself. All others qualify and stand in need. If the listener doesn't first "buy into" his or her separated condition and be open to seeking the remedy, there is little point in proceeding.

Next, the witness must point the way to the remedy. Salvation is provided through Jesus Christ, clear and simple! Numerous verses abound which describe God's plan through Christ. The witness can use a recommended verse, or his or her own favorite verse to describe God's wonderful plan of reconciliation through Christ. Regardless, the key here is sharing the plan with excitement! The believer hopefully need only recall his or her emotion when first converted.

The third point is a call to action. The best Gospel presentation in the world can be a fleeting emotional moment of little lasting value without an effective call to action. Romans 10:9-10 requires more than belief, it calls for action on the part of the new convert through verbalized confession:

> *"...if you confess with your mouth, 'Jesus Christ is Lord,' and believe in your heart that God raised him from the dead, you will be saved. For it is with your heart that you believe and are justified, and it is with your mouth that you confess and are saved."*

These basic principles of a Gospel presentation are an example of one effective way of sharing your faith. In Session Eight, our discussion will go into greater detail concerning a variety of techniques of sharing ones faith.

REVIEW BEFORE YOU GO AHEAD

1. Why are Bible study and meditation important for a growing believer?

   _____

   _____

   _____

2. List the main ingredients of a Gospel presentation.

   1) _____

   2) _____

   3) _____

V. KNOWING WHAT DISCIPLESHIP IS ALL ABOUT

At this stage of follow-up [establishing] the trainee is beginning to learn what discipleship is all about; it is the beginning of a vision for disciplemaking. Through what is being learned and through quality time with you, the trainee will start to see that *the result of being a functioning disciple is reproducing the reality of a walk with God in the lives of others*.

As the trainee continues and deepens in spiritual discipline, he or she will be impressed that these same disciplines can be reproduced in the lives of others. If the person is having a daily quiet time, the Christian can show another person how to have one as well; if he/she is taking sermon notes whose lessons are changing the person's life, the person can show another Christian how to do so also.

The continuing disciplines to which the new believer is now committed will include the following:

☑ Continuing sermon and study time notetaking.

☑ Continuing the daily quiet time and prayer.

☑ Starting and doing a weekly enriching Bible study.

☑ Continuing a Scripture memory program.

☑ Beginning meditation on all of the above biblical intake.

☑ Greater involvement in lifestyle evangelism through the local church.

The materials for the above deepening disciplines will be taken from whatever advanced follow-up or establishing "tools" the church is using. For other materials see the listing at the back of this book.

VI. MODELS FOR ONGOING FOLLOW-UP

A. The One-on-one Model.

If this discipleship training is being done in a one-on-one format, then each session between the discipler and the trainee will look something like this:

1. *Informal Conversation and "Catch-up" Time* (about 5-10 minutes).
2. *Discussion of Last Week's Devotional Assignments* (about 15-20 minutes). This will include sharing insights from sermon and education time notes, quiet time insights, recitation of Scripture memory verses, and meditation on passages of Scripture.
3. *Discussion of the Bible Study Assignment* (about 15-20 minutes). This will come from whatever Bible study booklet was chosen for this discipline.
4. *Discussion of the Reading Assignment(s)* (about 15-25 minutes). This segment will also include some additional instruction time on Christian character and evangelism.
5. *Prayer Time* (about 5-10 minutes).
6. *Weekly Spiritual Growth Assignment* (5 minutes).

This gives the discipler about 60 to 90 minutes time with his or her trainee. The order of the session can be varied throughout the approximately 10-12 meetings for follow-up. At the end of this period the trainee will be invited to continue for between six months and one year in an advanced discipling or equipping format.

B. The Small Group Model

A second option is available for this second stage of establishing — the small group. In this setting a well-trained instructor, who is a practitioner of the Christian disciplines discussed in this session, is leading a small group (about 6-12 persons) in the sharing of the devotional assignments, the weekly Bible study, the readings, and in learning new areas of the victorious Christian life.

Time will be more limited, for if this is a Sunday group, it will have about 45 to 60 minutes for each session. If it meets on a week night in a home, it will have more; if in some other public place during the week, it will have less time. Ground rules will need to be set, and the overall time extended to a church quarter or 13 weeks. This will be discussed in greater depth in Session 11.

Illustration of the Lesson

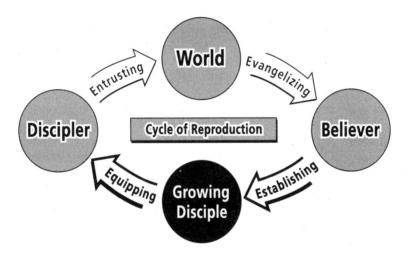

♦ *Ideas to remember*

The process here continues to be *establishing*, but is now at a deeper level. The spiritual disciplines continue from the earlier stage of follow-up, with new ones — Bible study and meditation — being added. Readings in textbooks and some instruction time also take place. Training in evangelism and personal witness are being carried out as well through the local church which the trainee now attends regularly. These disciplines include notetaking of all sermons and teaching times, the daily quiet time, weekly Bible study, regular Scripture memory, and meditation on the intake from all of the above.

Commitment to the local church is being strengthened, and a growing involvement in its ministry is taking place. The trainee is also beginning to catch the vision for spiritual reproduction or "multiplication evangelism." He or she is meeting regularly with a discipler or in a small group and is looking forward to the time of being able to assist another, a younger, Christian in growth to maturity.

Because this model is a biblical one, it will function effectively in any church setting and in any culture in the world.

Application of the Lesson

Here are some questions for reflection and application.

1. Following are the basic experiences that a growing new believer should have in this second stage of the establishing training. Check the ones that are currently present in the life of your disciple.

    ❐   Consistency in the Christian disciplines

    ❐   Regular biblical intake

    ❐   Character development

    ❐   Unashamed Witnessing

    ❐   Beginning of a vision for disciplemaking

    ❐   Deepening prayer times

2. What are some specific training objectives you can adopt which will help you balance your personalized Wheel Illustration?

3. Memorize 2 Cor. 5:17; John 15:7; and 1 John 3:21,22 in a Bible version of your choice.

Mentor Review

Congratulations again! You have finished the second unit of this course, building on the foundation of the first, and have carefully studied the biblical principle of establishing a new believer in Christ. It is time to meet with your mentor and review with him or her the biblical principles that are part of the establishing process for your follow-up and discipling ministry. Also *review the scripture memory verses* you have been learning the past several weeks.

During this time *share how things are coming along with the person you are now discipling*. Discuss any problems that may have developed in the relationship. Talk about your plans for the next few weeks. Before leaving pray together.

Unit Three:

Equipping Growing Believers

SESSION 7
Developing Character

Introduction to the Lesson

Edgar Guest had the ability to express himself well through writing. Here is a sample of his down-to-earth analysis of what Christian character must look like to others.

> ### SERMONS WE SEE
> I'd rather see a sermon than hear one any day;
> I'd rather one should walk with me than merely tell the way.
> The eye's a better pupil and more willing than the ear,
> Fine counsel is confusing, but example's always clear;
> And the best of all the preachers
> are the men who live their creeds,
> For to see good put in action is what everybody needs.

The Apostle Paul urged one group of Christians to follow the advice given by Edgar Guest in very short form: "Follow my example, as I follow the example of Christ" (1 Cor. 11:1).

The ministry of equipping growing believers involves two basic biblical principles:
1) Being an example to the growing believer as well as an instructor.
2) Teaching him or her to become a similar example to others in due course of time.

That is spiritual reproduction.

By way of review we might note that God has designed that redeemed people walk with him in newness of life. Just as physical babies need assistance in learning to walk, so spiritual babies do as well; just as they need help maturing, so do growing believers. So we can summarize the whole process:

Evangelism results in *believers* (converts).

Establishing results in *growing disciples.*

Equipping results in *disciplers*.

Where You Are in the Lesson

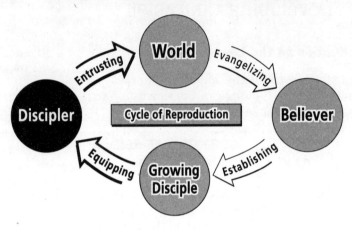

The ministry of *equipping*, begun in this unit, involves in-depth training and concentrates on the discipler as an example. Someone has well said…

> "Example is not just the best teaching method —
> it is the 'only' teaching method."

Goals for this session

1. You will know what is involved when you move from the establishing to the equipping stage in follow-up.
2. You will see the process of discipling growing believers so that they become spiritual reproducers.
3. You will realize what Christian character qualities are and how they can be built into the life of a disciple.
4. You will understand the necessity of being accountable and how to practice it.
5. You will learn to set priorities and to manage your time accordingly.

As you begin…

Listen to the messages for Session Seven (Cassette Tape 3)

The Lesson

When a new believer has been effectively followed up and has started growing spiritually, the time has come for a training process encouraging spiritual reproduction. This process may be called *equipping*.

An "older" and already maturing Christian should assist in the equipping process. Thus, the biblical concept of *equipping* may be defined as "the process of helping a maturing believer become fully prepared to assist another Christian to maturity and reproduction." The major goal of the training is to assure that every Christian make a unique contribution to the cause of Jesus Christ in this world.

I. THE PROCESS OF EQUIPPING

We have noted that Jesus spent the major part of his ministry in "private" — teaching and training a variety of smaller groups for service.

Jesus employed a strategy for world evangelization that would succeed. He chose a model of ministry that centered primarily on spending a large amount of time with twelve disciples. He made clear that the most effective spiritual reproduction occurs when we are able to transmit our mature walk with God to another person in such a way that the person can transmit that same lifestyle to another.

In patterning our ministries after Jesus', we arrive at the following emphases in the process of equipping:

1. We must *impart consistency of lifestyle*. This will be built into the trainee's life through the Christian disciplines, the example of the discipler, and through a team ministry.

2. We must assist in the *deepening of character development*. It will be necessary to work on specialized practical projects and develop peer accountability.

3. We must *convey the vision and philosophy of ministry*. This will come by reading quality books and spending meaningful time with the discipler.

4. We must develop *personal convictions for the ministry of disciplemaking*. This will develop through the instruction, advice, and example of the disciple's being initially involved in the training ministry itself.

5. We must enhance the *multiplication evangelism lifestyle*. It will occur only through participating in evangelistic outreach and through specific projects.

6. We must expand *Bible study skills directly from Scripture*. This comes about through learning and practicing inductive methods of study of the Bible.

7. We must provide *initial leadership training*. This will come about through opportunities for assuming responsibilities and decisionmaking and through the ongoing practice of the lordship of Christ in life and ministry to others.

8. We must help *deepen times of prayer* — individually, with the discipler, and in concert with other believers.

The result of the process is a maturing disciplemaker whom we can "entrust to teach others also" (2 Tim. 2:2).

II. GENERAL PRINCIPLES OF EQUIPPING

Overall the ministry of equipping is a form of leadership training because the man or woman walking with God will lead others in becoming functional disciples and spiritual reproducers. Some general principles apply to this process.

A. Principles for the Equipper

The *process is as important as the product*, so the discipler must know what to do with the trainee. This will include such principles as balancing gentle affection with firmness, structured instruction with unstructured modeling, and one-on-one time with group work and teamwork. It will include the impartation of vision, knowledge, and skills. When this "Discipleship Triad" (formulated by Mike Sabo of the Navigators) is examined carefully, the absence of one of the three will bring problems while the presence of all three will bring unity.

Vision + Knowledge – Skills results in *frustration*.

Knowledge + Skills – Vision results in *floundering*.

Skills + Vision – Knowledge results in *false doctrine*.

It is important to *tailor the job to the person* rather than the person to the job because of the individuality of Christians. If you try to tailor the person to the job, usually people will soon realize they are being used rather than helped in their training.

Remember that to disciple another person you must earn the privilege of doing so, and that discipling comes only from a relationship rather than a position. When a person asks you to help him or her grow in the Lord, they are paying you the highest compliment they can. They are putting their most prized possession in your care, namely their life. It is always a two-way street. Jesus called the disciples to follow him, and he would make them fishers of others (Matt. 4:19). They were to follow; his task was to make them to become fishers of men.

Truth and skills are always communicated best when they are presented simultaneously by teaching and example; the object is to build convictions in the trainee rather than merely performing assignments.

Selection is critical, so ultimately we are looking for men and women to train who are *F-A-I-T-H* Christians. This acrostic spells out the following character traits:

F = **Faithfulness** — commitment to carry out assignments
A = **Availability** — presence at all scheduled meetings
I = **Interdependence** — ability to work with others in harmony
T = **Teachability** — willingness to learn and be taught
H = **Holiness** — dedication to living the Spirit-filled life and practicing godliness

B. Principles for the Trainee

The person being discipled must understand that he or she is not "doing God a favor" by being a *F-A-I-T-H* Christian, but is living the *normal Christian life*. Willingness to be trained in ministry is the heart of this stage of maturing in our faith.

Since all Christian ministry is a people-to-people relationship, it is obvious that a disciple must develop a *heart for others*, following the compassionate example of Jesus (see Matt. 9:36). Those to whom we minister must know and *feel* that they are loved and cared for, that we are not merely carrying out a program for them and with them. We see Paul and his team in that role in Thessalonica (1 Thess. 2:7-8).

Our trainees must be convinced that the most effective way of fulfilling the Great Commission is through *spiritual multiplication*. This is a vision that cannot be only taught: it must be *caught* by your trainee. In its simplest form it is the vision for the potential of a single individual to become the one whom God uses mightily in his work in the next generation. Every person we train has the possibility of becoming a future Paul, John Wesley, or Hudson Taylor. See Paul's concern for this in his report to the Corinthians (2 Cor. 2:12-13).

At the heart of all our people ministries must be a *servant attitude* (see 2 Cor. 4:5), for we serve God by serving others (Mark 10:45). It is not something that comes naturally to us, so it must be carefully developed.

The church of Jesus Christ is a team effort, not a haven for isolated individuals. As was true in the early church, every disciple today must develop the ability to function effectively as a *member of a team*.

Another quality is a *volunteer spirit*. Jesus gave his life willingly for us; we must be just as willing to give our lives for the sake of others. In the spirit of Isaiah, "Here am I! Send me!" (Isaiah 6:8), is the fulfillment of love in practice: "Greater love has no one than this, than to lay down one's life for his friends" (John 15:13, NKJV).

Here Am I! Send me!

Isaiah

Have you volunteered yourself to God to place you daily for effective ministry?

To teach others how to walk with God and to encourage them to grow spiritually in Christ, we have to *set the example*, imperfect though it may be. On a number of occasions Paul said something like, "Be imitators of me as I am of Christ" (1 Cor. 11:1; see also Phil. 4:9). Humble men and women, who are pursuing holiness and practicing godliness, can indeed serve as living examples of spiritual growth.

More and more we must show effectiveness in our witness. Even though we may not be evangelists, we are to be men and women who *naturally and effectively share our faith* with others daily. Both life and word must show the indwelling Christ.

In this stage of discipling the trainee may be given the opportunity to *become a Bible study leader*. Through diligent study, prayer, and practice any Christian can become an able Bible study group leader, not a teacher, but one who can lead a Bible study by skillfully using questions to stimulate group discussion.

Another skill that should be cultivated in this stage of training is a *genuine sensitivity to people*. To minister more effectively to the needs of others around us, we must be attuned to their needs. This is a skill that can be developed if we make the effort to do so. Ultimately this skill is the fulfillment of Paul's exhortation: "Let each of you look out not only for his own interests, but also for the interests of others. Let this mind be in you which was also in Christ Jesus" (Phil. 2:4-5, NKJV).

Finally, trainees should learn how to *think for themselves*. They learn to use their powers of observation, think through what they have observed, read, or heard, and come to proper conclusions on the basis of that data.

To summarize, here are the characteristics that should be growing in genuine disciples' lives:

• heart for others	• spiritual multiplication
• servant attitude	• member of a team
• volunteer spirit	• set the example
• naturally and effectively share our faith	• become a Bible study leader
• genuine sensitivity to people	• think for themselves

C. Strategy for Implementation

How do we go about building these character qualities and skills into the life of another? Simple, we follow the strategy used by Jesus and duplicated by the early church:

1. Be sure that your trainee is established as a functioning disciple of the Lord Jesus Christ and is consistent in the basic disciplines that lead to spiritual growth (see Sessions 4 — 6).

2. Involve your trainee in a ministry for which the individual is being equipped by spending time with the person in discipling meetings and also in ministry (see Mark 3:14).

   ☑ First, assist the person to become involved in your ministry by providing the individual with *occasions* to *watch* you serve, in which the individual can eventually *participate*, and ultimately *perform*.

   ☑ Second, help the person develop and succeed in his or her *own* ministry by learning to *see* opportunities for service with a team from your church. (Team members supplement and complement each other's unique gifts.)

☑ Third, help the person develop and succeed in his or her *own* ministry by learning to *develop* opportunities, then follow through with ministry (with or without a team).

☑ Fourth, *expose* the person to *other individuals* who have strengths in areas where you might be weak. We reproduce in kind—not only our strengths, but also our weaknesses. This "cross-training" will help the disciple become more balanced in life and ministry.

3. Equip your trainee for service in accordance with his or her spiritual gifts. You must assist the person to discover, develop, and use these God-given gifts. Discernment, through observation and prayer, is needed on the part of the trainer. Discovery by the trainee of his or her spiritual gifts will come through prayer, observation, hindsight, and involvement.

REVIEW BEFORE YOU GO AHEAD

1. How can we distinguish between *establishing* and *equipping*?
   _____
   _____

2. Why are vision, knowledge, and skills so important as a unity?
   _____
   _____

3. What is a F-A-I-T-H Christian?
   F - _____
   A - _____
   I - _____
   T - _____
   H - _____

4. Stop for a moment and ask yourself, "Am I a faith Christian? Why or why not? Think deeply about your answers.

III. CHARACTER DEVELOPMENT

No two books nor any two disciplers will have the same comprehensive list of what character qualities should be built into one's life. So the suggestions here emphasize scriptural priorities in the Christian life. The major thrust is to build toward godly character and a holy lifestyle.

The building of godly character qualities in the trainee's life is a conscious effort on the part of both the discipler and the trainee. Godly character does not just happen; it must be prayerfully and continuously developed. This is what Paul advised Timothy:

> *"Don't let anyone look down on you because you are young, but set an example for the believers in speech, in life, in love, in faith and in purity. Until I come, devote yourself to the public reading of Scripture, to preaching and to teaching. Do not neglect your gift, which was given you through a prophetic message when the body of elders laid their hands on you. Be diligent in these matters; give yourself wholly to them, so that everyone may see your progress. Watch your life and doctrine closely, persevere in them, because if you do, you will save both yourself and your hearers" (1 Tim. 4:12-16).*

This text gives us some principles for character development in a person who wants to live a life pleasing to the Lord. Our speech and the way we live daily show others what we really are. Godly character may be seen by others in the visible attributes of love, faith, and moral purity.

Godly character is strengthened and fed by our being in the Word of God by every means available (see Session 6) and through an active ministry to others. Diligence and wholeheartedness are visible marks of a developing godly character, and everyone can see the progress we are making.

But we must be on constant guard against our enemy, the devil. He would try to detour us from our efforts to build godly character and love to ruin our testimonies and ministries. We have to watch closely both our actions in daily life and what we believe or think. We must determine to persevere in building these qualities, which may require daily and immediate choices we might have to make. The grand result is that we will grow in godliness and be used by him to help others do the same. That is because God is "in the business" of changing the lives of his people (*sanctification*), both ours and those to whom we minister.

The procedure in this equipping ministry in the area of character development might be summarized in the following principles of teaching and training:

♦ *Authority*. Everything we say and do must be based on the Word of God. The trainee must recognize that Scripture is the ultimate authority.

♦ *Repetition*. In many cultures today and in the rabbinical teaching of Jesus' time repetition was the major means of teaching.

♦ *Clearness*. When we teach and train others, we must be sure that our communication is simple, clear, and understood by the trainee.

♦ *"On-Your-Own."* When we "allow" our trainees to discover the necessary lessons for themselves, they learn and apply these lessons more quickly and effectively.

♦ *Love*. We teach and train in love. The trainee must know and feel that his or her welfare is the chief concern of the discipler. "The object of all instruction is to call forth that love which comes from a pure heart, a clear conscience and a sincere faith" (1 Tim. 1:5, TCNT).

The responsibility of the discipler is to create a climate most conducive to learning and applying biblical truth. By God's grace and the power of the indwelling Holy Spirit we can help our trainees root out the negative sinful qualities of bitterness, hostility, fear, "idols," improper responses or reactions, and ungodly imaginations.

We should follow the instruction that Paul gave Timothy: "correct, rebuke, and encourage" (2 Tim. 4:2).

♦ *Correction* is primarily the work of the Holy Spirit in our lives through Scripture.

♦ *Rebuke* is when we assist the trainee to respond to the correcting of the Spirit of God.

♦ *Encouragement* is absolutely necessary in any teaching/training ministry.

This kind of character-building will result in a trainee becoming a strong disciplemaker in time. God gets all the glory for that development.

IV. THE NECESSITY OF ACCOUNTABILITY

One of the major problems the church has had and still has is the failure of some leaders to be accountable to anyone. *If we are not accountable to someone, we become easy prey for the enemy to lead us into pride and self-sufficiency.* From the very beginning of the biblical record, when Adam was made accountable to God on the issue of the knowledge of good and evil (Genesis 2), this issue has been a major problem among people and nations. Since the Christian is especially accountable to God, the built-in safeguard that the Lord has for his church is accountability to one another.

A. Accountability in the Church

The structure of the ministry of the Lord Jesus Christ shows the accountability principle in operation. Jesus was accountable to God the Father, "I have glorified you on the earth. I have finished the work which you have given me to do" (John 17:4, NKJV). In a way, too, he made himself accountable to the disciples. The disciples in turn were accountable to Jesus, "And the apostles, when they had returned, told him [Jesus] all they had done" (Luke 9:10a, NKJV).

It is interesting to note that the great Apostle Paul, so often working on his own, reported regularly to his accountability group. After the first mission he reported back to the church which had sent the team out earlier, "When they [Paul and Barnabas] had come and gathered the church together, they reported all that God had done with them" (Acts 14:15, NKJV). After his third mission he returned to Jerusalem and gave a report of his ministry to James and the elders, "On the following day Paul went in with us to James, and all the elders were present. When he had greeted them, he told in detail those things which God had done among the Gentiles through his ministry" (Acts 21:18-19, NKJV).

The writer to the Hebrews commands his readers (then and now), "Obey those who rule over you, and be submissive, for they watch out for your souls, as those who must give account" (Heb. 13:17, NKJV). Depending on the form of church government your local assembly or denomination has, some form of accountability should be evident . When Christ brought the New Testament church into being, he established it so that there is a leadership structure and accountability. We as individual Christians are accountable to our leaders; in the same way in a discipling relationship the trainee is accountable to his or her discipler, while the equipper is in turn accountable to the trainee by modeling the Christian disciplines before his trainees.

B. Accountability to Jesus Christ — Now and Later

Ultimately, however, we are all accountable to God and to his Christ. In many parables Jesus clearly taught this truth (read Matt. 24:45-51; 25:14-30; Luke 16:1-13; 19:12-27; 20:9-18). The Apostle Paul is the one who expounds on this topic in two significant contexts. To get some perspective on this important teaching we must tie together some significant passages of Scripture.

- ◆ Ephesians 2:10—"For we are God's workmanship, created in Christ Jesus to do *good works*, which God prepared in advance for us to do" (NIV, emphasis added). It is God's will for believers to do good works.

- ◆ Romans 14:10b,12—"For we [believers] will all stand before God's judgment seat ...So then, each of us will give an *account* of himself to God" (NIV, emphasis added). We believers are held accountable for our works, whatever they might be.

- ◆ 2 Corinthians 5:10—"For we [believers] must all appear before the judgment seat of Christ, that each one may *receive* what is due him for the things done while in the body, whether good or bad" (NIV, emphasis added). At "the judgment seat of Christ" we believers will receive what is due us according to God's standards—our reward (or lack of it).

- ◆ 1 Corinthians 3:12-15a—"If any man builds on this foundation [Christ] using gold, silver, costly stones, wood, hay or straw, his work will be shown for what it is... If what he has built survives, he will receive his *reward*. If it is burned up, he will suffer loss; he himself will be saved" (NIV, emphasis added). Whatever we do with our Christian lives, we will either receive a reward or lose that reward.

The issue in these Pauline statements is *not* eternal security (destiny) in the judgment or good works or rewards; the issue has to do with our accountability for what we have done or not done with our Christian lives. Commands given to us (for example, Rom. 12:9-21; 1 Thess. 5:12-22) must be obeyed; for that obedience or disobedience we will be held accountable. We are also the possessors of many privileges (Eph. 1:3). However, with these privileges come responsibilities (for example, Eph. 4:1–6:20) for which we will be held accountable.

C. Confronting with Care

Among the "one another" responsibilities we have toward fellow believers is the one which says, "Admonish one another" (Rom. 15:14; Col. 3:16; see also 2 Thess. 3:15). Greek scholars tell us that the original word essentially means "to show what is wrong." Its basic idea is to seek earnestly to influence the mind and will of another person by suitable instruction, exhortation, warning, and correction. But we must be very careful how we admonish or correct an erring brother or sister; we must follow Paul's clear teaching to speak the truth in love (Eph. 4:15). Practical suggestions include:

1. Prayer for the situation.

2. Confront constructively and accurately. Use terms such as "It seems to me," "It looks like," and "It appears that…" This will allow them to explain and perhaps set the discipler straight.

Because I love you, I will tell you the truth in love.

Confronting with Care

3. Attentively listen to the other person.

4. Inform the other person on what the Bible has to say regarding a problem and give the person a way to start correcting it.

5. Continue in prayer.

6. Correct patterns in a person's life rather than isolated incidents; major on the major issues. In every instance leave the person with hope and encouragement.

7. Be careful not to assume an authoritarian, "know-it-all" approach. Christ alone is the authority, and you must keep the focus on him at all times.

V. SETTING PRIORITIES

We have already noted that discipleship means *discipline*, and one of the vital areas of life where self-discipline must be exercised is in our setting of priorities. The word "priority" indicates that some things come "*prior*" or "*before*" other things, not necessarily *in place of* other things. A list of priorities is simply a list of what things are most important in your life, and in what order. The list does not necessarily indicate the *amount* of time you spend on each item, but how much you *value* it. For example, if we truly believe that having a daily quiet time is an important priority, then we will set aside time to have a meaningful experience with the Lord.

We cannot borrow, save, hoard, or buy time; we can only spend it. We spend it wisely or foolishly. If we are to spend it wisely, we must submit our time to the lordship of Jesus Christ: "Lord, what do you want me to do with my time for you?" Management of time, then, is vital to a disciple's total lifestyle. Furthermore, every one of us has exactly the same amount of time each day; how are we going to use it for the Lord?

Setting priorities correctly falls under the larger topic of managing ourselves, for that has to do with the proper stewardship of one's calling by the Lord, what we are and what we have — time, talent, and treasure. We must set

Spend Time Wisely

our priorities for utmost personal development and maximum productivity for God.

The biblical basis for our setting priorities correctly is found in Paul's letter to the Ephesians: "Be very careful, then, how you live — not as unwise but as wise, making the most of every opportunity [redeeming the time, KJV], because the days are evil. Therefore, do not be foolish, but understand what the Lord's will is" (Eph. 5:15-17, NIV). These observations can be made about this teaching:

♦ We are to be careful in our use of time and set priorities for our use of it.

♦ We are to make the most of the time we have, setting our priorities to take advantage of every opportunity.

♦ We must be on guard against the evils of our times, not letting our priorities get under the control of Satan.

♦ We must practice the stewardship of time because that is God's will for us.

♦ The key to all of the above is to *commit* each priority each day to God during our quiet time with him (Psalm 118:24; 90:12).

Some practical suggestions for time management would include learning better ways to do what you are already doing, learning to do the important rather than the seemingly urgent, learning to distinguish between the essentials and the electives. Make a list of your priorities for a given day, then do them one at a time, practicing the N-O-W formula:

N =Do it *NOW*!

O =*ONE* thing at a time.

W =*WELL* done.

♦ *Ideas to remember*

Both *teaching* (the impartation of facts, ideas, and concepts) and *training* (the impartation of learned skills) are necessary during the equipping process. This stage of discipling is designed to build godly character qualities and ministry skills in the trainee's lifestyle. Following a discussion of principles needed in the discipler's life and the trainee's life for this stage to be effective, the rest of Session 7 suggested various ways to build character. (Ministry skills will be dealt with in Sessions 8 and 9.)

Character development was discussed from Paul's teaching of Timothy (1 Tim. 4:12-16), from which six important principles were gleaned. The Session concluded with a discussion on accountability and the setting of priorities.

Application of the Lesson

Here are some questions for reflection and application:

1. Have you ever listed out your priorities? Reflect on the following sample list and then write out your list of priorities:

    A Sample Priority List:

1.	Relationship with God	(1Cor. 1:9; Mark 12:30)
2.	Relationship with Family	(1 Tim. 3:4–5; Titus 1:6)
3.	Ministry	(Matt. 28:18:–20; Eph. 2:10)
4.	Job	(1Tim. 5:8; 2Thess. 3:10)
5.	Personal Development	(Luke 2:52)

    Your Priority List:

1.	
2.	
3.	
4.	
5.	

2. Memorize Romans 8:16; Psalm 90:12; and 2Peter 1:5-8 in any version of your choice.

SESSION 8
Sharing Your Faith

Introduction to the Lesson

An artist, seeking to depict on canvas the meaning of evangelism, painted a storm at sea. Black clouds filled the sky. Illuminated by a flash of lightning, a little boat could be seen disintegrating under the pounding of the ocean. Men were struggling in the swirling waters, their anguished faces crying out for help. The only glimmer of hope appeared in the foreground of the painting, where a large rock protruded out of the water. There, clutching desperately with both hands, was one lone seaman.

It was a moving scene. Looking at the painting, one could see in the tempest a symbol of mankind's hopeless condition. And, true to the Gospel, the only hope of salvation was "the Rock of Ages," a shelter in the time of storm.

*But as the artist reflected upon his work, he realized that the painting did not accurately portray his subject. So he discarded that canvas, and painted another. It was very similar to the first: the black clouds, the flashing lightning, the angry waters, the little boat crushed by the pounding waves, and the crew vainly struggling in the water. In the foreground the seaman was clutching the large rock for salvation. But the artist made one change: the survivor was holding on with only one hand, and with the other hand he was reaching down to pull up a drowning friend (Robert E. Coleman, **The Heartbeat of Evangelism**, pages 7-8).*

One of the great tragedies of the modern age, particularly in the church in North America and Western Europe, is that so few people among those who consider themselves Christians regularly share their faith. Somewhere during the past century our adversary has convinced many even in Bible-believing churches that it is all right for you to be a non-involved Christian, only attending church and Sunday school, supporting missionaries far away, but without reaching out in your local community.

Excuses are many: "Not enough time"; "I might be rejected"; "People don't want religion pushed on them." They go on and on. It is sad to see the annual statistical report of denominational growth and see so many have a row of zeroes under the column "Additions by Adult Profession of Faith." Some churches have not added anyone through conversion for years.

As has often been true in church history, the work of the church of the Lord Jesus Christ is being done by very few of his followers. We seem to be satisfied in this century in the western world to leave the task of evangelism to just a few of the more dedicated saints. It is discouraging for some pastors to hear their people say, "Don't talk to us about evangelism. That's what we hired you to do!"

The Bible, which is the inspired Word of God, teaches in no uncertain terms that the responsibility to witness is the task of *every believer* — without exception. Ultimately it is to be our response of gratitude for the so great salvation we have received through Christ. It is the essence of the picture described above — one drowning person having found refuge helping another drowning person to that refuge.

Where are you and where is your church regarding sharing your faith? The call of God to his redeemed people of all ages is that they become the channels of the great salvation of God to all people and nations. A growing disciple will seek to carry out this mandate. A disciplemaker by example will teach others how to do it.

Goals for this session

1. You will see the biblical mandate of witness or evangelism as the responsibility of every believer.

2. You will be a practitioner of evangelistic outreach through the church, and a personal witness for Christ.

3. You will know how to train another person through motivating him or her to share his or her faith.

4. You will learn how to instruct another person in various ways of sharing his or her faith.

5. You will transmit your witnessing skill through personal sharing with your trainee and with teams in the church.

6. You will begin seeing the whole world, both the local community and "the ends of the earth," as God sees them, and to plan a strategy for doing your part in reaching out.

As you begin...

Listen to the messages for Session Eight (Cassette Tape 4)

The Lesson

It is imperative that we train growing and maturing Christians in sensitive and winsome witnessing. This training must include motivation, procedural instruction, and actual practice — going out and doing it. All of which must lead to a commitment to sharing our faith actively the rest of our lives here on earth. This means we must think in terms of an evangelistic *lifestyle*.

Obviously if we are to disciple the trainee in these areas, we must ourselves, as equippers, be practitioners. If we are to motivate and help others to share their faith, we must already be doing so. Thus this session will deal not only with what to teach and train but also some strategies of sharing our faith in Christ *together*.

I. THE BIBLICAL MANDATE FOR EVANGELISM

The biblical revelation emphasizes one concept repeatedly. The people of God are to tell others about the God who is their Lord and Savior. From the Fall to the Second Coming of Christ, God's people are always to be involved in evangelism, and this responsibility falls into the area of obedience to the God who has redeemed them. It is purely an expression of our love to Jesus and gratitude for what he did for us. This mandate of God may be seen throughout Scripture. It begins in creation, extends through the chosen people, Israel, and culminates in the life of Christ and his church.

We have seen in an earlier chapter that the Great Commission is recorded for us in five different passages: Matt. 28:18-20; Mark 16:15; Luke 24:46-48; John 20:21; and Acts 1:8. These passages apply to all believers, and set forth the task in which we are to be involved until Christ returns.

The writers of the letters of the New Testament pick up this same concern, urging new generations of Christians to lovingly obey the divine mandate.

♦ Paul — **"Be ambassadors!"** Every person who is a "new creation" in Christ is also an ambassador for Christ telling others about him (see the whole context of 2 Cor. 5:11 — 6:2).

- The Book of Hebrews — **"Run the race!"** All Christians are in a race in this world, and we are to invite others to join us in that race (see the context of Heb. 10:22-25; 12:1-2; 13:13, 16).

- James — **"Do good works!"** The very essence of doing good works is doing something that will benefit others. The greatest good work is to tell others the good news of salvation through Christ (see the context of James 1:19, 22; 2:14-17).

- Peter — **"Be ready to answer everyone!"** We are to know the Gospel so well that we can spontaneously answer anyone who asks us about our faith in Christ (see the context of 1 Peter 3:13-16).

- John — **"Tell what you have seen and heard!"** A dynamic daily fellowship with the Lord Jesus must result in a winsome witness. (See the context of 1 John 1:1-3.)

- Jude — **"Snatch them out of the fire!"** The Christian who is in the Word, praying regularly, and committed to obedience, will share his/her faith with others, in easy or difficult situations (Jude 20-23).

II. WHY WE MUST SHARE OUR FAITH

We are to share our faith for three reasons: *gratitude*, *compassion*, and *obedience*, all which flow out of *a love for Christ*. In gratitude for the great salvation we have received by grace through faith we want to run out into our world shouting to all who will listen, "Look what the Lord has done for me! Look what he can do for you!" We want to share the great gift of salvation with the rest of the world.

We share our faith because of genuine compassion for the lost. When we realize that human beings without Christ are *perishing*, we have taken the first step toward developing genuine compassion for them. Furthermore, our daily walk with Jesus through the Word and prayer should develop in us what is on his heart. He had great compassion for the mul-

Sharing our Faith

titudes who were like sheep without a shepherd (read Matt. 9:36-38; 10:5). That kind of compassion can only develop when we have spent much time alone in the presence of Jesus.

We share our faith because we want to obey our Lord. The obedience we render to our Savior is not that of a slave to a master, but the loving and willing obedience we give to the one who loves us with an everlasting love. It is interesting to note that in the New Testament obedience and love are always tied together. We obey because we love.

♦ *"If you love me, keep my commandments"* (John 14:21).

♦ *"He who has my commandments and keeps them, it is he who loves me"* (John 14:21).

♦ *"If anyone loves me, he will keep my Word"* (John 14:23).

♦ *"If you keep my commandments, you will abide in my love"* (John 15:10).

♦ *"This is my commandment, that you love one another as I have loved you"* (John 15:12).

♦ *"These things I command you, that you love one another"* (John 15:17).

Why must we share our faith? Because we want to please him who has saved us from our sins, because we see humans dying without the Lord, and because we want to show the reality of our love by obeying him.

REVIEW BEFORE YOU GO AHEAD

1. Sum up the Great Commission in your own words. Let your definition reflect your particular situation.

   _____

   _____

2. What does the rest of the New Testament have to say about the Great Commission?

   _____

   _____

   _____

3. Why do you believe you should share your faith?

_____

_____

_____

III. MEANS OF SHARING OUR FAITH

If we are convinced that we should be sharing our faith regularly, then how do we do it? According to the Scriptures the means by which we witness is by telling others a word of truth, a personal testimony of what the Lord has done in our lives, with the Word of God at its very core (see Romans 10:17).

A. Sharing a Word of Truth

This form of witness is sharing a true but partial presentation of the Gospel. "The first thing Andrew did was to find his brother Simon and tell him, 'We have found the Messiah!'" (John 1:41, NIV). Andrew told his brother a fact, but did not go through the details of a Gospel presentation. We can do this in our many short encounters with people in such a way that they will know that we believe in God, that we are Christians and disciples of Jesus. Then as the Holy Spirit uses that word of truth in their lives, they might ask us about Christ on the next occasion.

B. Sharing a Personal Testimony

This form of witness may be given in three ways:

1) A *conversion* testimony

2) A *profession of faith* testimony

3) A testimony to *what God has been doing* in our lives lately.

In each case we share with others what God means to us and how he has worked in our lives.

A *conversion* testimony recounts the time and place you received Christ as Lord and Savior. It basically follows a three-point outline:

1) what my life was like before coming to Christ;

2) what happened in my coming to Christ;

3) what my life is like now with Christ at its center.

With this in mind, write out your testimony for a 3-minute presentation, approximately 300 words. Edit, then rewrite it. Memorize it to present to anyone who will listen to you. (A good model to study is what Paul said in Acts 22:3-21 and 26:1-28.)

A *profession of faith* testimony usually is given by those who were raised in a Christian home and may not know the precise time and place when they were converted, but came to a clear assurance of salvation in Christ. Write this testimony out also, edit it to three minutes, then learn it well to present to others.

A testimony of *what Christ has done for me lately* shows others that God is alive, well, and active in the lives of people today. This can be such things as a specific answer to prayer, God's protection from harm in some miraculous way, or the enablement God gave to ask forgiveness for some wrong done to another person and how both of you were strengthened by that experience. It should be anything that shows God really working in your life right now.

C. Sharing the Plan of Salvation

Many Gospel presentations are available today to be used in a variety of different situations, with diverse kinds of people, and in various cultures and nations. You should learn a presentation that communicates well in your culture.

The main point in all presentations is to highlight the main facts of human life, destiny, and God's provision of redemption, which comes to us by grace through faith. Remember that it is not our persuasiveness that brings people to Christ, but the Spirit of God using the Word of God and convicting persons of sin, righteousness, and judgment (John 16:7-11). We are but channels for the Holy Spirit to work through. Still, it is our responsibility to present the facts of Scripture well. The power is not in the presentation or in the one doing the presenting — but in the Gospel (see Romans 1:16).

IV. SOME SUGGESTED GOSPEL PRESENTATIONS

Here are a few Gospel presentations. They are printed in easily obtained tracts.

A. "Steps to Peace with God"

The Billy Graham Evangelistic Association has written a tract that has been used effectively around the world. It is short, pictorial, and the pertinent Scriptures have been written out. The best way to use this tract is to take someone through it; walk the person to whom you are witnessing through the four steps suggested in it.

☑ *Step One* is discovering and realizing that God's plan for each person is peace and life (Romans 5:1; John 3:16; John 10:10). If this is God's plan, why are most people not having this experience?

☑ *Step Two* is acknowledging that humankind's problem is a separation from God (Romans 3:23; 6:23). People have chosen to disobey God and go their own willful way. A holy God cannot stand the presence of sin, so a great separation has taken place. (A picture shows a great gulf fixed between God and people with people's attempts to bridge it.) Some have tried to bridge this gap by good works, religion, philosophy, and morality, but none of these attempts deal with the problem of sin. What is the remedy for sin?

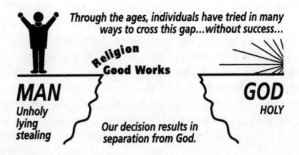

Through the ages, individuals have tried in many ways to cross this gap...without success...

MAN
Unholy
lying
stealing

Religion
Good Works

Our decision results in separation from God.

GOD
HOLY

☑ *Step Three* is recognizing that God's remedy is the death of Jesus Christ on the cross of Calvary (Romans 5:8; John 14:6; Eph. 2:8-9). That is the only way the sin problem can be resolved, for when Jesus died on that cross and rose from the grave, he paid the penalty our sins deserved. (Another picture shows the gap between God and people bridged by the cross of Jesus.) God has provided the *only* way, so how does an individual cross over the gap bridged by the cross?

☑ *Step Four* is making the proper response of receiving Christ as Lord and Savior (Rev. 3:20; John 1:12). We must believe (trust) that Jesus' death and resurrection take care of our sin problem, then receive him into our hearts and lives by personal invitation. Is there any good reason why you cannot receive Jesus Christ right now?

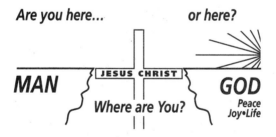

The rest of the booklet presents four additional items: (1) What the inquirer needs to do to receive Christ; (2) a suggested sinner's prayer; (3) God's assurance that the prayer is heard (Romans 10:13; 1 John 5:12-13); and (4) five suggestions on how to deepen the relationship just begun.

B. Other Presentations

Many other Gospel presentations are available today to the person who wants to be an effective witness for Jesus Christ. Nearly all denominations and churches with active evangelistic outreach have a presentation that fits their ministries. Many of these use some variation of the Bridge Presentation (see Appendix D).

C. Leading in A Sinner's Prayer

After presenting the plan of salvation, then ask, "Does this make sense to you?" Ask, "Would *you* like to receive Jesus as your Lord and Savior right now?" If there is something standing in the way, then deal with it. Often the answer will be something like: "Yes I would if I only knew how." At this point ask the person to repeat the prayer below after you. (It incorporates the ingredients of responding to the Gospel and a person's becoming a Christian.)

A Sinner's prayer

"I am a sinner and I am sorry for my sins.   [Confession]

I want to turn from my sins; I am willing to begin a new life with your help.   [Repentance]

Lord Jesus, I believe you died for my sins on the cross.   [Faith]

Please come into my heart and life right now and save me.   [Invitation]

From this moment on my life belongs to you and you alone. I will love you, serve you, and tell others about you; I will trust you to live your life through me.   [Consecration]

Thank you for coming into my life and forgiving my sins today. Amen."   [Thanksgiving]

After the prayer ask if the person understood clearly what was said, and did the words truly express the desire of his or her heart.

REVIEW BEFORE YOU GO AHEAD

1. What are three means of sharing our faith?
    1) _____
    2) _____
    3) _____

2. What are the three kinds of personal testimony?
    1) _____
    2) _____
    3) _____

3. List 4 steps to peace with God:
    1) _____
    2) _____
    3) _____
    4) _____

V. GETTING STARTED

Now that we know what our responsibilities in witness are, how do we get started?

A. Begin Where You Are

If you have never done this regularly before, **now** is the time to get started. Study and memorize the instructions above and begin immediately sharing your faith by using "Steps to Peace with God" or the Bridge Illustration. If you need to receive some training yourself, seek out an experienced soul-winner, and go calling together. There should be some people like this around, probably within your church.

When you are ready to be a model to your trainee, do some things together where he or she can see you share your faith. Later you can talk about the experience and what can be learned from it. The next time let your trainee take the initiative while you assume a support role.

B. Going With a Team

Local church visitation teams provide an excellent occasion for learning how to share your faith effectively. Such teams usually have 2-3 persons, led by someone with experience in evangelism. You will most likely visit persons who have attended a church service, are new in the community, or live in close proximity to the church.

Those just beginning in evangelism can observe the approach of the more experienced witness in such items as introducing the team at the door, stating the purpose of the visit, steering the conversation to spiritual things, and briefly communicating the Gospel. The leader can gradually encourage the other members of the team to participate by quoting a verse of Scripture, sharing their testimony, and eventually the Gospel message.

C. Preaching an Evangelistic Sermon

For a preacher, of course, this is an expected ministry. There are occasions, though, when members of the congregation can bring an evangelistic message with great effectiveness. If help is needed in developing this form of public communication, a companion course to this one, titled *Evangelistic Preaching,* is obtainable through the Billy Graham Center Institute of Evangelism.

VI. DEVELOPING STRATEGIES FOR WITNESS & EVANGELISM

A variety of excellent opportunities exist for churches in their outreach into their communities. The local situation, of course, will determine which methods are the most effective. Whatever the Spirit of God uses to help someone get to Christ is a good method. Utilize those most suited to your needs. Some methods that might be considered include:

- ❐ *Family tree evangelism* is the deliberate effort to reach family members with the Gospel. Discipler and trainee strategize together on how that can be done most effectively.

- ❐ *Evangelistic letter-writing* is presenting the Gospel through correspondence with friends and family members far away. A loving, prayed-over letter, with the Bible verses written out, can be an effective way of sharing your faith with people far from your present residence.

❐ *Hospital visitation* is sharing your faith in a hospital while visiting friends or family members who are hospitalized. You can do this with nurses, roommates or wardmates, and even in other rooms or wards by permission of the sick person.

God loves you.
May I pray for you?

Hospital Visitation

❐ *Home visitation* involves visiting persons in their home for the purpose of answering their questions and sharing the Gospel with them.

❐ *Friendship evangelism* involves a longer time by getting acquainted with neighbors, work associates, and friends, developing a friendship, and waiting for the opportunity to present the Gospel in a low-key manner.

❐ *Evangelistic Breakfasts, lunches or dinners* involve inviting non-Christians to a meal for fellowship with Christians and to hear a speaker talk about how the Christian faith relates to everyday life.

❐ *Evangelistic films* are excellent tools to expose non-believers to the Gospel. These films can be shown in your home, at the church, or in any other suitable location.

❐ *Evangelistic meetings* provide occasions where Christians can bring their unsaved friends to hear the Gospel preached.

❐ *Evangelistic Bible studies* in small groups provide a non-threatening atmosphere where people can be exposed to the Gospel message.

♦ *Ideas to Remember*

This session has dealt with the important topic of being a witness for Christ and sharing your faith with a person who is not a believer in Jesus Christ. It began with a presentation of the biblical mandate for witness or evangelism, and the overwhelming teaching of Scripture that *every* Christian has the responsibility to be a witness for Christ. It is gratitude for our salvation, compassion for the lost, and our love for Christ that compels us to obey his commission.

We noted three means of sharing our faith:

1) Word of Truth.

2) Personal Testimony.

3) Gospel Presentation.

We then examined briefly Billy Graham's "Steps to Peace with God," and how to lead another person in a Sinner's Prayer. We offered some suggestions on how to get started and how to plan evangelistic outreach in a local church were given. The stewardship you now have is to get started!

Application of the Lesson

Here are some questions for reflection and application:

1. Write down why you are convinced that the Scriptures call on all believers in Christ to share their faith in him.

2. Name three people you believe God wants you to share the Gospel with over the next few months.

   1) _____

   2) _____

   3) _____

3. Using the principles learned in this session, suggest a strategy through which you will share Christ with these three people.

4. How can you and your trainee go on evangelism calling through your church?

5. Memorize 1 John 1:3; 2:5; 2 Timothy 1:12 and John 20:21 in a Bible version of your choice. Review all your verses.

SESSION 9
Becoming a Discipler

Introduction to the Lesson

One of the great practitioners of and writers on prayer in the early 20th century was E. M. Bounds. His best-known work is *Power Through Prayer*, and although written primarily for pastors or preachers is nevertheless applicable to *every* Christian. At the beginning of that book he wrote:

> *We are constantly on a stretch, if not on a strain, to devise new methods, new plans, new organizations to advance the Church and secure enlargement and efficiency for the Gospel. This trend of the day has a tendency to lose sight of the man or sink the man in the plan or organization. God's plan is to make much of the man, far more of him than of anything else. Men are God's method. The Church is looking for better methods; God is looking for better men (emphasis added; "men" here can be taken in the generic sense for all Christians, male and female; quoted from the Zondervan [1962] edition, page 11).*

If that was true at the turn of this century, how much more does it apply to the church in the latter part of the 20th century? Organizations and programs have become primary and people have become secondary in many churches. This was one of the great problems of the Christian church when it emerged from its era of persecution and became legal in the Roman Empire (during the time of Emperor Constantine, in the early AD 300s). People became faceless masses, eventually stifling evangelism and discipling. Ultimately, this trend led to the distinction between clergy and laity, wherein the individual layperson was to be seen and not heard.

In Scripture the individual is important. Note, for example, the huge number of names recorded in the Old Testament; note Jesus' ongoing concern for and dealing with people as individuals; note the mention of over 100 names in the Book of Acts; note the constant reference to individuals in the writings of Paul (Rom.16:1-16 and 2 Tim. 4:9-16). From the very beginning of human history and throughout the story of redemption in the Bible, people as individuals have been important to God.

Programs may come and go, but people are forever. Aside from God and his holy angels only three things will last beyond this world as we now know it, love, his Word, and the human soul. Organizations, buildings, monuments, and programs will disappear. The century in which we live seems to have lost sight of that in the church; what we hear emphasized over and over again is bigger programs, methods, organization, administration and buildings.

But to God the worth of the individual is primary. God has chosen human beings, made in his image, created male and female, to be the ones through whom all his work on earth is to be done. The best evangelism is person-to-person evangelism; the best discipling is person-to-person discipling. The only effective way to get something done in and through the church is through people.

So the best strategy we have available to us in Scripture and through Jesus' example is men and women evangelizing and discipling other men and women. Those who have become disciples of the Lord Jesus and have grown and matured in their walk with him must reproduce that reality in the lives of others. Every disciple must become a discipler and by God's grace reproduce the actuality of his or her walk with God in the life of another.

This is not to say that the corporate aspects of our lives and ministries must be ignored or abandoned. The best way to work with individuals is in the context of the Christian community — the church — as we will discuss in Sessions 10 and 11.

Goals for this session

1. You will understand the objectives of the equipping/entrusting ministry with your trainee.

2. You will appreciate that the "finished product" of the discipling process is a disciplemaker.

3. You will pray about a person or persons to train in leadership.

4. You will strategize a discipling ministry in your church.

5. You will begin implementing that ministry in your situation.

As you begin...

Listen to the messages for Session Nine (Cassette Tape 4)

The Lesson

Scripture enables us to see what it is that God expects of us at the conclusion of the "formal" discipling process. Paul expressed it well in his letter to the church at Colosse:

"So, naturally, we proclaim Christ! We warn everyone we meet, and we teach everyone we can, all that we know about him, so that, if possible, we may bring every man up to his full maturity in Christ. This is what I am working at all the time, with all the strength that God gives me." (Col. 1:28-29, Phillips)

Paul's great desire for those to whom he ministered was their growth to Christian maturity. This parallels human development, for what parents having raised their children to maturity do not anticipate becoming grandparents when these grown children marry? In the same way Christian disciplers look forward to the day when their trainees have matured enough to begin having their own spiritual children and raising them to maturity. What a thrill it is for faithful disciplers to meet their new spiritual grandchildren!

I. OBJECTIVES FOR THE EQUIPPING MINISTRY

In the equipping process we move more and more from a discipler/trainee relationship to a partnership in the ministry and mutual accountability relationship. To summarize what was listed in Session 7 (Section I, "The Process of Equipping") we see the major objectives in this last stage of discipling to be

- ☑ enabling your trainee to have his or her spiritual disciplines become more and more habit patterns and part of an overall Christian lifestyle. These will no longer be assigned, but expected as part of a disciple's life.

- ☑ assisting your trainee in developing Bible study skills that will eventually enable the person to dig out of the Scriptures God's lessons for life (application-centered).

- ☑ contributing to your trainee's character development by planning and doing specific practical projects together. (See Session 7 on character development.)

☑ being involved with your trainee as a partner in evangelism and calling on unbelievers through your local church's outreach ministry.

☑ deepening your prayer lives by spending quality time together praying for yourselves and each other's intercessory concerns and participating with others in "concerts of prayer."

☑ continuing to strengthen your trainee's vision for disciplemaking (spiritual reproduction) so that the disciple can in turn pass on that vision to others.

Since the second stage of the equipping process [*entrusting*] is a form of leadership training, certain practical objectives need to be considered and imparted as well. Many of these are actually extensions of what has already been worked on in the establishing process and in the first stage of the equipping ministry.

Most of these are self-explanatory and all may not be needed by every potential discipler. So you will have to be selective in your equipping ministry, using only the ones your trainee needs. Add to them or delete as necessary, then adapt the others to fit each individual trainee's needs.

Depth in life and ministry is a lifelong process. All of us should be growing spiritually and ministering more effectively throughout all of our lives. All of us need to be sensitive to whatever ministry God may call us in life, and this may be lifelong or in segments (during a lifetime a person may have been a pastor for 15 years, a teacher for 10, and a missionary for the rest). Included in this calling is the use of the spiritual gifts the Holy Spirit has given us, which we have discovered, developed, and used for God's glory (more on these in Session 10).

Again, throughout all of our lives we should be working on building up our strengths and correcting our weaknesses. Leadership training would include such areas as attitudes, listening to others before making decisions, practice under limited supervision, and a readiness to accept suggestions from persons seeking to help us be our best.

Give your trainee assignments that are designed to stretch his or her faith and make that person more dependent on the Lord. Give varying practical ministry assignments to refine skills, then follow up on these with a debriefing session (see the example of Jesus in Mark 6:3). Assist in learning how to discern between "the tyranny of the urgent" and a carefully planned ministry, and to know when to say "Yes" and when to say "No."

Help your trainee learn good communication methods and build a solid doctrinal foundation for his or her life and ministry. The latter comes through getting to know the Bible and its teaching very well, for doctrine and practice are inseparable.

II. CHARACTERISTICS OF A DISCIPLER

What does the "finished product" look like? This is a question we can ask both of ourselves and those whom God gives us to equip for ministry. A discipler above all must know how to be filled with the Holy Spirit and live visibly the victorious Christian life (or whatever your tradition prefers to call it). Other characteristics and attributes should be present as well.

A. Filling with the Holy Spirit

It is crucial that a discipler understands, practices, and teaches others the filling of the Holy Spirit. God can only use Spirit-filled men and women in the ministry of discipling, for we reproduce what we are far more than what we say or teach. Without the filling of the Spirit we are living and ministering in the flesh, that is, in our own wisdom, abilities, and strength.

This ministry of the Spirit is accomplished in us when we are yielded to God without reservation and fully trust his Word. It is the only ministry of the Spirit that we as believers are commanded to appropriate for ourselves in concert with all other Christians. The terminology of filling is found in these passages: Luke 1:15, 41, 67; Acts 2:4; 4:8, 31; 9:17; 13:9; Luke 4:1; Acts 6:3; 7:55; 11:24; 13:52; Eph. 5:18.

Paul's teaching in Ephesians is a word of command: "Let the Holy Spirit fill you" (NEB). Three conditions are given throughout Paul's writings for our obedience to this command:

1. *"Do not quench the Spirit"* (1 Thess. 5:19). To quench the Spirit is to refuse to follow his leading and to resist doing his will clearly revealed in his Scriptures. It is saying "No" to him.

2. *"Do not grieve the Spirit"* (Eph. 4:30). To grieve the Spirit is to persist in sin and to do that which we know to be wrong. Because God cannot have fellowship with those who continue in sin, grieving the Spirit results in the loss of spiritual fellowship and closeness with him, and our prayers will not be heard (Psalm 66:18).

3. *"Walk in the Spirit"* (Gal. 5:16, 25). Positively, to walk in the Spirit is to be yielded to him, to have all sins confessed, and to live in obedience to his commands in Scripture. It is to be in step with him in all of life, and it is to be an ongoing experience for the believer (present tense).

B. Other Characteristics

Among the key characteristics for an effective discipling ministry are:

1) personal holiness (1 Thess. 4:3-4; 5:23; it is God's will for us).

2) a passion to see the honor of God advance through all of life, even if it means suffering temporary dishonor or loss (1 Cor. 10:31).

3) a commitment to take up one's "cross" (Luke 9:23; John 16:33; 2 Tim. 3:12). To carry our cross is to follow Jesus whatever it takes.

Take Up Your Cross

4) living in an attitude of thanksgiving and praise to God (Eph. 5:19-20).

The discipler should try to see everything from God's perspective:
"We are asking God that you may see things, as it were, from his point of view by being given spiritual insight and understanding. We also pray that your outward lives, which men see, may bring credit to your master's name, and that you may bring joy to his heart by bearing genuine Christian fruit, and that your knowledge of God may grow yet deeper" (Col. 1:9-10, Phillips).

He or she also needs to have the courage "to die right rather than live wrong," that is, no compromises with the world and be willing to see others advance at his or her own expense, for promotion comes only from the Lord (Psalm 75:6-7, KJV). The discipler should learn to make eternity judgments instead of time judgments:

"He [Moses] considered the 'reproach of Christ' more precious than all the wealth of Egypt, for he looked steadily at the ultimate, not the immediate, reward" (Heb. 11:26, Phillips).

Other characteristics that should be visible in a discipler are maintaining a positive outlook (even when things go wrong—Phil. 4:8, 13), a determination to keep going in spite of obstacles, relating well with non-Christians, and getting along with people in the church.

All of this involves making right decisions. Life is made up of choices and decisions: Receiving God's salvation, having a quiet time, memorizing Scripture, being honest, maintaining moral purity, practicing obedience to God and his Word, and all our relationships with people. Indecisiveness in people usually reveals immaturity, lack of getting all the facts, fear of consequences or people, lack of convictions, and *at root a lack of faith*.

REVIEW BEFORE YOU GO AHEAD

1. What are the major objectives in this second stage of the equipping ministry?

_____

_____

_____

_____

2. In your own words, what is being filled with the Holy Spirit?

_____

_____

_____

_____

3. What are some of the spiritual and practical characteristics that should be visible in a discipler?

_____

_____

_____

III. HOW TO SELECT PEOPLE TO DISCIPLE IN THE EQUIPPING PROCESS

The essential qualities of a person ready to be equipped for ministry leadership are the five ingredients of being a *F-A-I-T-H* Christian (see Session 7, Section II-A); these are faithfulness, availability, interdependence, teachability, and holiness. Such a person would be willing to learn and put into practice what was being learned.

One source for such people is the whole follow-up and discipling process. A person who was followed up and established properly in both stages (Sessions 4 & 6) and who has been equipped for ministry (Sessions 7 & 8) is now ready for training in leadership (Stage Two of the equipping process). This person has already demonstrated the qualities of a *F-A-I-T-H* Christian.

Another source is people in the church who already have a walk with God that is consistent and regular, but have never received any training in ministry. They have learned how to walk with God but have never been challenged or confronted with the call to reproduce the reality of that walk in the lives of others. The pastoral staff and other leaders may know of such people to whom an invitation to be discipled and equipped for ministry would be an answer to prayer.

A third source is a congregation-wide invitation for members to make themselves available for training in discipling or leadership. The qualifications and prerequisites might be printed in a communication vehicle (bulletin, newsletter, public announcement) that would draw out some people the leadership may have otherwise never considered.

From whatever source potential trainees may come, they must be fairly confronted with the *costs* of such a personal ministry (read Jesus' parables on counting the cost of discipleship, Luke 14:25-33). For the person who is already a committed disciple of Jesus, the costs are not the basis on which he or she will choose to enter training; knowing the costs simply previews what the ministry entails (see 2 Cor. 5:9).

The ministry of disciplemaking will cost you, among other things:
♦ Time.
   ♦ Inconvenience.
      ♦ Pressure to live the life of a disciple, not just to teach about it.
         ♦ Vulnerability.
            ♦ No recognition (this in not an "up-front" ministry).
               ♦ Emotional pain and hurt.
                  ♦ Disappointments.

But this ministry also has numerous rewards:
- Knowing you are pleasing God by doing his will.
    - The joy of walking in holiness.
        - A clear conscience.
            - Seeing growth and progress in your trainee.
                - Seeing fruit in your spiritual grandchildren.
                    - Helping build the body of Christ.

What more do we really need?

Persons drawn to this training can be assigned to an experienced discipler. The disciplers arrange meeting times for both individual and group sessions. A member of the pastoral staff or a layperson should take on the responsibility for coordination.

IV. STRATEGIES IN THE TRAINING PROCESS

The primary strategy in the equipping process is creating a vision for multiplication evangelism, or spiritual reproduction. This vision is not so much taught as it is caught from another person. We must create the climate in our ministry so that the trainees catch that vision. The primary strategy breaks down into two principles.

A. The Principle of Multiplication

If we are to be convinced of the need for spiritual reproduction in our churches, we need to understand and appreciate the principle of multiplication. It is basically the mathematical function of geometric progression. Envision a checkerboard. If you place one grain of wheat on the first square, two on the second square, then double that number for each square, how many grains of wheat would there be on the 64th square?

The answer, of course, is so astronomical that a number would be mind-boggling. There would be enough wheat on that 64th square to cover the entire subcontinent of India several feet deep. This example simply shows the *power* of multiplication versus the slower method of addition. Project that illustration now to see the power of spiritual multiplication.

If your church had a member with the gift of evangelism who led an average of one person to Christ per week, who then joined your church, you would welcome an additional 52 members a year through the efforts of one church member. That is 520 people in ten years, considered excellent church growth.

But what if you had another member in your church who was so gifted that he led a person to Christ each day? If they all joined the church, that would mean 365 new members each year through the efforts of one person, and you would have

The Principle of Spiritual Multiplication

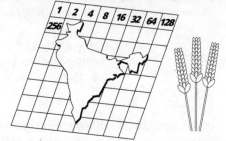

Enough wheat to cover the subcontinent of India several feet deep!

to have a new building program every three or so years, for you would have 3,652 new members in a decade.

But you also have another person in your church whose ministry is not so visible. She leads a person to Christ, then disciples the individual for a year, and the two of them each lead another to Christ, so at the end of two years you have four new members from this "slow" ministry. But they keep on reproducing. At the end of another year the four become eight, then 16 by the end of the fourth year. If this ministry continues, by the end of the 33rd year 8,589,934,592 people have been won to Christ *and* discipled, which is far over the population of the whole world!

Impossible? Probably so, but *theoretically* possible, for it shows the power of spiritual multiplication. It is an obvious *ideal*, and breakdowns can occur all through the process, but it is still the greatest potential the church has of reaching our world with the Gospel in this generation. Wouldn't you like to be part of this reproductive process?

B. The Principle of Infiltration

Because this ministry of establishing and equipping is done quietly and not before all the media publicity, its results have a tendency to affect communities, societies, organizations, and even nations. That's the way the early church did it, for they infiltrated the Roman Empire with real Christians. Here is a contemporary illustration.

In 1975 a committed Christian woman went to work for the Philippine government's Forestry Research Institute (FORI). Twelve years later a Filipino Christian organization made this report: "In 1975 S_____ knew of only three Christians in FORI. Today there are 1,000 employees in 15 offices around the country. 95% of the employees have heard the Gospel and 60% profess to know Christ as Savior, and Bible studies thrive. Christians are occasionally ridiculed for their faith and honesty, but administrators value their work. They can be trusted, work hard, and get along well with their co-workers."

This kind of story is being repeated in a number of other government agencies in the Philippines and in other nations in the world. Some of the great upheavals of the late 1980s and early 1990s in Eastern Europe and the growth of the Christian movement in the Republic of China were the results of infiltrative evangelism. A careful study of the strategy of the Apostle Paul in all his ministry shows how that style of ministry succeeded. It is still reproducible today.

REVIEW BEFORE YOU GO AHEAD

1. How do we go about recruiting trainees for an equipping ministry in the local church?

_____

_____

_____

2. What existing qualities do you look for in people who are ready to be trained in discipling?

_____

_____

_____

3. From the following list of costs and benefits, check those you have experienced:

COSTS	BENEFITS
❏ Time	❏ Knowing you are pleasing God
❏ Inconvenience	❏ The joy of walking in holiness
❏ Pressure to live the life of a disciple	❏ Seeing growth and progress in your trainee
❏ Vulnerability	❏ A clear conscience
❏ Emotional pain and hurt	❏ Seeing fruit in your spiritual grandchildren
❏ Disappointments	
❏ No recognition	❏ Helping build the body of Christ

V. CONDUCTING THE REGULAR MEETINGS

The format for discipling remains essentially the same for this stage as it was in Session 6, Section VII. In the equipping ministry the following three formats should be considered.

A. The One-on-one Time

One-on-one time is a necessary part of this stage since more intimate matters will be involved. Regularly scheduled meetings, lasting about two hours each, should go on for about 20 weeks or five months. The composition of each meeting should include:

1. *Unstructured Fellowship* (about 5 minutes).

2. *Scripture Memory Recitation and Review* (10 minutes).

3. *Discussion of the Bible Study* — moving from the question-and-answer format to the "on-your-own" directly from Scripture (15-20 minutes).

4. *Discussion/Interaction with Disciplemaking Readings* (15 minutes).

5. *Working on Personal, Evangelistic, and/or Character Building Projects* (45 minutes).

6. *Prayer Time* (15 minutes).

7. *Weekly Spiritual Growth Assignment* (5 minutes).

The order is flexible and can be changed for variety's sake. Toward the end of the training, the teaching will be more and more in leadership, the second stage of the equipping

B. The Group Meetings

At this stage group meetings are not an option but a necessary addition. Periodically, [twice a month] disciplers and their trainees will meet in small groups to begin planning and working on team ministries (see more on this topic in Session 11). Team ministries are required in the equipping process and are comparable spiritually to special forces training in the military.

These sessions will teach teamwork and involve disciples working with other disciples in a variety of ministries in and through the local church. Additional leadership training can also be included.

C. The Ministry Team

At the group meetings the trainees will be organized into evangelism teams for local church ministry. These teams will be sent into the community and other cities and countries as opportunities become available.

The continuing illustration shows how the person who has gone through the whole establishing/equipping process is now trained and able to reproduce the whole ministry.

The Completed Cycle of Disciplemaking

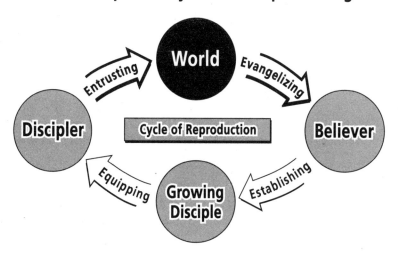

♦ **Ideas to Remember**

The process here is *entrusting*, with a strong emphasis on leadership training. The objectives of this ministry are *to produce a self-starter who is dependent on the Holy Spirit and able eventually to disciple another Christian to reproduce spiritually.* By way of summary six objectives were listed:

☑ Deepening of spiritual disciplines

☑ Developing inductive Bible study skills

☑ Working on character development

☑ Involvement in evangelistic outreach

☑ Prayer times with the discipler

☑ Strengthening of the vision for disciplemaking

We discussed a variety of practical objectives that would be of assistance to the trainee in future ministry. The 'finished product' of *equipping* and *entrusting* a disciple is a person who is filled with the Holy Spirit, and one who visibly shows a variety of additional characteristics.

We discussed suggestions concerning how people in a local church might be challenged and recruited to become trainees in this ministry of discipling. We also discussed the costs and rewards of this ministry. Understanding the principles of spiritual multiplication and infiltration of a given society or nation is important for the disciple to "catch the vision" of the power of effective disciplemaking.

We introduced the modified discipling format to include group meetings along with one-to-one training, and we also discussed how to conduct team ministries.

Application of the Lesson

Here are questions for reflection and application:

1. Evaluate yourself based on the following objectives for the equipping ministry.

	Strong	Average	Weak
Deepening of spiritual disciplines	❏	❏	❏
Developing inductive Bible study skills	❏	❏	❏
Working on character development	❏	❏	❏
Involvement in evangelistic outreach	❏	❏	❏
Prayer times with the discipler	❏	❏	❏
Strengthening a vision for disciplemaking	❏	❏	❏

What can you do to strengthen your weak areas?

_____

_____

_____

_____

2. How do you teach another person how to be filled with the Spirit?

3. How can you transmit the vision of multiplication to others?

4. Memorize Psalm 119:11; 2 Tim. 2:2; and Eph. 5:17-20 in a Bible version of your choice.

Mentor Review

It is time again to meet with your mentor and review what you have learned in the past three lessons and what you may have been doing in your ministry of discipling. You should review with your mentor all the application questions of the past three lessons, as well as the content of what you have learned, including your scripture memory verses.

You have been disciplining at least one person. Now it is time to involve that person in the process of discipling another person. The place to begin may be in the initial follow-up of a new Christian, or with someone he or she knows is looking for direction. Discuss this together.

You have now studied all the principles of discipling another person so that he or she becomes a discipler as well. The last unit will deal with the use of that ministry in the local church, for that is the ideal place for discipling to occur. Plan strategies with your mentor on how best to introduce this ministry to your church leadership.

$\mathcal{U}$NIT FOUR:

Developing
a Discipling Church

141

SESSION 10
Assimilation in the Church

Introduction to the lesson

Churches are always looking for the perfect pastor. David Haney humorously describes the ideal pastor as one…

> who preaches exactly twenty minutes and then sits down. He condemns sin, but never hurts anyone's feelings. He labors from 8 AM to 10 PM in every kind of work, from preaching to custodial service. He makes $60 a week, wears good clothes, buys good books regularly, has a nice family, drives a good car and gives $30 a week to the church. He also stands ready to contribute to every good work that comes along.
>
> The ideal pastor is twenty-six years old and has been preaching for thirty years. He is at once tall and short, thin and heavy-set, and handsome. He has one brown eye and one blue; his hair is parted in the middle with the left side dark and straight and the right side brown and wavy. He has a burning desire to work with teenagers and spends all his time with the older folks. He smiles all the time with a straight face because he has a sense of humor that keeps him seriously dedicated to his work. He makes fifteen calls a day on church members, spends all his time evangelizing the unchurched, and is never out of his office (*The Idea of the Laity*, page 42, Zondervan, 1973).

How wonderful it would be if every pastor could approximate that vivid description of the ideal as perceived by church members. But reality for the vast majority is a long way from this. God has given many godly and able pastors to many churches, but they are ordinary human beings saved by grace through faith. They are generally very committed to the work of the ministry, but they cannot possibly do all that needs to be done by themselves. Developing a disciplemaking ministry that reproduces itself is the best way to multiply the pastor's effectiveness.

If every pastor were to follow the example of the Apostle Paul and surround himself with a team of disciples, begin training them in a church context, then have them function in ministry with him...then we just might see churches operating more closely to the biblical model of the New Testament.

The biblical model is a team ministry. Jesus himself gave us the clearest example in the varying groups he had around him for some three years (see Session 2). That team model is seen vividly in Paul's ministry throughout Luke's record (Acts) as well as in the constant mention of people around him in his letters.

This chapter will suggest that the discipleship model discussed in the earlier sections of this study course should be integrated into the ministry of the local church. It is the ideal model for assimilating new members into a church that is active in outreach evangelism. It is the model that allows the greatest spiritual growth to occur in the shortest time to produce committed and active church members and future leaders in that congregation.

This is not to suggest that all the programs of the local church are to be tossed out and new programs instituted in their place. This session is suggesting, however, that *the discipleship model be appended as a **ministry** to existing successful programs to complement and supplement them in their effectiveness*.

Goals for this session

1. You will appreciate the church as "the body of Christ," and realize how important the church is to the individual Christian and the individual believer to the church.

2. You will know how to discover, develop, and use your spiritual gifts for the benefit of those in the church and in its outreach.

3. You will understand the process of assimilation and be prepared to participate in that ministry in the church.

4. You will visualize the discipleship model of ministry as an integral part of all the other ministries of the church.

5. You will recognize that each church must find the model of disciplemaking that works best in their situation.

As you begin...

Listen to the messages for Session Ten (Cassette Tape 5)

The Lesson

Flowers and plants grow best in the ideal climate of a prepared soil, enjoying consistent weeding and the right amounts of sun, temperature, and rain. Disciples grow best in the ideal climate of a loving fellowship of Christians, enjoying consistent instruction in such subjects as "putting off" negative character qualities and "putting on" positive character qualities, along with the right amounts of love, care, and "exercise" (doing ministry).

In his letters to the Ephesians and Colossians, the Apostle Paul imparts specific instruction regarding what we are to "put off" and "put on" in our spiritual growth to maturity (Eph. 4:17-32; Col. 3:5-17). Disciplers assist their trainees in applying Paul's instruction within the context of other believers in the local church or assembly. That is the ideal setting for spiritual growth: younger believers seeing older believers as role models in the growth process.

I. THE CHURCH AS THE BODY OF CHRIST

Among the many images or metaphorical descriptions of the church, the most memorable and easiest to understand is that of "the body of Christ." This image for the church is the most frequently used and the best developed in Paul's writings.

Paul instructs the Corinthians regarding the unity and diversity of the body of Christ (1 Cor. 12:12-27). The body is one, but within it are *feet, hands, ears, eyes, and noses*, each set in the body as God pleased. These, of course, refer to the spiritual gifts of members of the body. Additionally, leadership gifts and the mandate for gifted leaders to equip all the saints for their individual works of service must be included (Eph. 4:1-16). The body functions at its best when all members are involved, serving Christ according to the gifts they have been given.

All God's people throughout the world and throughout time are the body of Christ. Every local congregation is a visible manifestation of this body in a given locality. One way to visualize the concept is to draw a parallel from the human body.

In the human body, two relationships are key for proper functioning. One relationship regards the body to the head, which issues orders and sets the body in motion. The second relationship pertains to each part of the body and its interaction with the other parts. It's tough to get nourishment from your digestive system without your hands shoveling the food in your mouth!

Not only does the body of Christ concept imply a living *relationship* of believers with Christ, but it also emphasizes that the church is a *living* and *growing* organism. As such, the church must grow; it is to grow internally by building up fellow believers in Christ, and it must grow externally through the proclamation of the good news to the outside world.

The Church Body

The body of Christ image challenges individual Christians to be part of the local expression of that body so they can do their share in the work. When people are led to Christ, they must be incorporated into the body as quickly as possible if they are to grow and mature into spiritual reproducers. One-on-one discipling alone cannot produce reproducers because they need the "discipling" of the whole body as well.

Individuals must contribute their gifts to the well-being of the whole; simultaneously, the body collectively contributes to that individual's personal growth to maturity. Through caring for one another, every part (individual) of the body grows, and, as a whole, ministers for Christ.

REVIEW BEFORE YOU GO AHEAD

1. Answer the following true-or-false questions by writing T or F in the blank space which corresponds to the question:

___ (a) The biblical model for ministry is team ministry.
___ (b) To implement a discipleship program, all the old programs of the church should be tossed out first.
___ (c) According to 1 Corinthians 12, some members of the body are insignificant, so it doesn't matter whether or not they function.

2. Why is the local church an ideal setting for a new believer's spiritual growth?

_____

_____

_____

_____

II. SPIRITUAL GIFTS

Some believers will respond to various parts of the training process faster than others, and become better able to carry out certain ministries. Such is the strength, beauty and diversity of the body of Christ. The pastor, teacher, and discipler need to be sensitive to this fact when making decisions regarding which gifts a growing Christian in a church may or may not have.

The biblical data on spiritual gifts is found primarily in four significant passages in the epistles. The major teaching is in 1 Corinthians 12–14, while the others are in Romans 12, Ephesians 4, and 1 Peter 4.

What spiritual gifts have you been given?

❏ Wisdom	❏ Evangelizing	❏ Pastoring
❏ Faith	❏ Teaching	❏ Apostleship
❏ Healing	❏ Serving	❏ Leadership
❏ Prophecy	❏ Tongues	❏ Knowledge
❏ Encouraging Others	❏ Administration	❏ Miraculous Powers
❏ Showing Mercy	❏ Helping Others	❏ Discernment

The expression *spiritual gifts* comes from a combination of words that speak of *gifts of grace*, not something earned or bought; they come from and through the Holy Spirit. To clarify further, a spiritual gift is a special attribute given by the Holy Spirit to each member of the body of Christ according to God's grace and will.

Each believer should know what his or her spiritual gifts are because they will enhance the person's spiritual life. They will help the believer personally know God's will; and their discovery will ultimately strengthen the whole church. It is imperative that believers discover, develop, and use their spiritual gifts for their God-ordained purpose of benefiting the body.

Faithful servants of Christ need to know in what ministry they should be serving (see Mark 10:42-45; Matt. 8:21-23; Luke 12:42-48). Furthermore, they are expected to be good stewards of what gifts Christ has given them for their ministry because they will be held accountable for that stewardship (see Matt. 25:14-30; Luke 19:12-28; 1 Cor. 4:1-2; 1 Peter 4:10-11).

Practically speaking, some positive results of the awareness and use of the spiritual gifts present in your congregation are:

♦ Each member will know what to do best in the church.

♦ All members will be able to work together in greater harmony and effectiveness, avoiding disagreements and quarrels, self-centeredness, and pride.

♦ The whole body will mature and grow spiritually.

♦ God will be glorified.

How, then, do we discover, develop, and use our spiritual gift or gifts? Here are four suggested steps to assist Christians in determining which gift/gifts they have [or don't have]. Once determined, the believer then becomes responsible before God to develop these gifts and use them for the welfare of the body of Christ.

1. *Explore the Options*: Prayerfully go through the passages of biblical gifts, form your own opinions, and establish your own philosophy. First you need to know what each gift is and which gifts you know you don't have.

2. *Examine your Own Feelings:* How good do you feel about exercising this particular gift? If you don't, it may be an indication that you do not have this gift. You should exercise your gift joyfully and with satisfaction.

3. *Evaluate your Effectiveness*: Remember that spiritual gifts are for the benefit of the whole body of Christ. When you use your particular gift or gifts, you should see some positive results. What activities does God appear to be blessing in your life?

4. *Expect Confirmation from the Body:* Others in the body must recognize these gifts in us by seeing the effectiveness and benefits of them, and so confirm them to us. What do mature Christians believe your gift(s) to be?

It is the responsibility of the discipler in the establishing and equipping process to make sure that the trainee has the opportunity to exercise his or her spiritual gifts. If further help is needed in discerning one's gifts, see the appropriate section in the Bibliography (Appendix F).

III. THE ASSIMILATION PROCESS

People who have been led to Christ must be brought into the life of the local church. Often this involves church membership. This *process* of assimilation takes time to incorporate new people into what is already a comfortable group of people who know each other and work well with one another. The critical issue for effective assimilation is making sure that the new person feels wanted, realizes growth in this setting, knows love and care from others, and will be able to do something in the church in the future.

People whom we have contacted or who have come as guests ("visitors") to the church must come to the place where they say to themselves, "I would like to be a part of *this* church and *these* people. I would like to *belong* here!"

This is where effective follow-up and discipling fit in. The public ministry of the church plus the ministry of the discipler create the ideal climate for maximum growth and learning. While the church provides the worship celebration, teaching of the Word of God, and acceptance within a loving and caring group, the discipler provides the explanations, the modeling, and the encouragement to keep on going. The group also provides additional models of a Christian lifestyle, so that the trainee sees many people walking with God and actively growing in their faith.

The key to the assimilation process is the whole congregation knowing that new Christians are constantly coming into the life of the church and consciously creating a climate in which these young believers can grow and thrive spiritually.

REVIEW BEFORE YOU GO AHEAD

1. What do you think are your spiritual gift(s)?

_____

_____

_____

2. What can you do to make the church more effective in the assimilation of new believers?

_____

_____

_____

IV. INTEGRATING THE DISCIPLESHIP MODEL INTO YOUR CHURCH

How do you integrate the discipleship model discussed in sessions 1 through 9 into the ministry of the local church? Since in most cultures the pastor is the key leader in a local congregation, it is vital that this undershepherd of the flock of God know, understand, and be 100% behind this ministry. The discipleship model is *not* a replacement for any of the usual programs and ministries in a local assembly; it is actually an enhancement to the existing programs.

Those trainees who come through the whole of the discipling ministry will eventually be used as leaders in all the other ministries. With what they have learned and with the training they have received they will be able to function in nearly every ministry a local church has. They will be able to work with youth, with adults, with elderly, and reach out to various kinds of people in the immediate community around the church.

The discipleship model (see Session 9) has the most potential for growth and reaching the world with the Gospel in this generation. It is modeled on the team ministry Jesus had with the apostles and disciples that was so effectively copied by the early church.

Some practical suggestions for integrating the discipleship model into your church might include the following:

1. Don't make major changes too quickly. A slow and deliberate approach is best in the long run.

2. Begin by discipling a few people without drawing undue attention to the process. The result is what counts.

3. Work with the leadership in defining the biblical purposes and goals of the church ("Church Mission Statement").

4. Expect the church leaders to be examples to the people in making disciples. Begin training those who are faithful, available, interdependent, teachable, and committed to a life of holiness (*F-A-I-T-H* people).

5. Begin using those who are being trained in follow-up of new Christians, discipling of older Christians, and in the ministry of evangelism either in one-on-one or group settings.

V. DIFFERENT CHURCH MODELS OF DISCIPLEMAKING

As pastors and church leaders have discovered the principles of disciplemaking and sought to apply them in their specific context, different models have emerged. This is what we would expect to happen, for while the principles of discipling do not change, the methods used to implement these principles can and must change as the context for ministry changes.

Many good models of disciplemaking in the local church exist. Some churches utilize a *one-to-one approach,* linking up each new believer with a "spiritual friend" to help guide the new Christian in the early days of his or her spiritual life. The actual procedure used to pair up the new believer with a more mature believer varies widely. Some churches rely on a church member to initiate contact and take the new believer under his or her wing. Because oftentimes this seems to let new converts "fall through the cracks," many churches have a staff member or a trained layperson who draws from a group of potential disciplers to assign a more mature believer to each new Christian. Some large churches have elaborate systems of record-keeping which allows the person who oversees the disciplemaking ministry to "match" new converts with disciplers who share certain characteristics: e.g. age, marital status, occupation, and hobbies. Detailed information forms are kept on file for each trained discipler in the church so his or her characteristics can be matched as closely as possible with those of the new convert. While having one or more of these characteristics in common are not essential for a successful discipling relationship, they can help provide a foundation for a deep and lasting friendship.

The planned number of meetings between the discipler and the new believer and the content for these meetings again varies widely from church to church. Some churches use materials furnished by their denomination or another Christian group to guide them through the process. Other churches "tailor-make" their materials to fit their particular context. The principles discussed earlier in this course will help guide the church in its decisions in these matters.

A few churches provide this spiritual friend not only to new Christians, but also to each new member who joins that particular fellowship. Again, surveys can be utilized to "match" new members with someone in the church that shares common interests. This ministry of encouragement can be utilized no matter where the new member is in spiritual maturity. We all need support and help from other believers. Studies show that friendships are often the "glue" that keep persons active and involved in a local fellowship.

Other churches follow a *small-group approach.* These groups can take numerous and varying forms. Some churches offer a class for new believers. This class focuses on basic spiritual growth and orients the new Christian to life as a Christian and as a church member. Oftentimes this class is taught by the pastor, though it can be just as effective (if not more so) when taught by a layperson in the church.

Some churches utilize the educational system of the church to place new Christians in follow-up and discipleship groups with people of similar age. In other churches the entire membership is divided into groups which meet in homes. New believers are placed into one of these groups where they receive support and encouragement. The possibilities of small groups are endless.

You might consider either of these basic approaches for your church, or some kind of combination of the two. Each church needs to discover a discipleship structure suited for its particular context. God may lead your church to pattern your structure after something another church has done, or he may lead you to create a new "wineskin." Always keep in focus that methods can and must change — but principles do not change.

The illustration on the following page shows how the three components of one-to-one, small group, and large group all work together to further the ministry of the church.

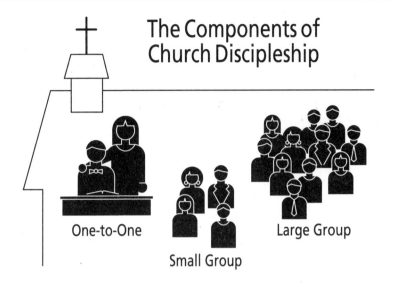

The Components of
Church Discipleship

One-to-One

Small Group

Large Group

♦ *Ideas to remember*

Jesus Christ brought his church into being to create the ideal climate in which his new and older followers could have the maximum opportunity to grow, to flourish as Christians in this world, and to carry out the mission assigned to them. Through history the church may never have come up to that ideal, but an active church of any generation can approximate the biblical model through a committed membership. At the heart of that commitment is discipleship as discussed in the first nine sessions of this course.

This session studied the biblical teaching on the church as the body of Christ, noting that all of its members or parts must contribute to the well-being of the whole. The discipleship model is the best way to train all the people of the body to walk with God and to minister according to their respective spiritual gifts. Thus the second section of this lesson noted the relationship of the individual to the church and the church to the individual.

The key to the proper functioning of people within the church as disciples of the Lord is to discover, develop, and use their spiritual gifts to the glory of God, the building up of fellow believers, and in ministry to the world. Again the discipleship model is ideal for their development and use within the body and in outgoing witness to others.

We also studied the issue of assimilation; new believers need a good context in which to grow and to learn how to minister. The discipleship model offers a means by which effective assimilation can be carried out in the local church committed to following the pattern of a biblical ministry.

Attention was also given to the means by which a discipleship model might be integrated into the ministry of the local church. Any plan must have the full support of the pastoral leadership, wholehearted approval by the governing board, and ownership by the church body. Finally, it was noted that both one-on-one and small group approaches to disciplemaking can be incorporated into the program best suited to a local church's context.

Application of the Lesson

Here are some questions for reflection and application:

1. How would you help your disciples discover, develop, and use their spiritual gifts?

2. Based on this session, if you had total freedom to implement a discipleship model in your church, what would it look like?

3. Memorize Eph. 4:3-6; Heb. 10:24, 25 in a Bible version of your choice.

Session 11
Discipleship Groups

Introduction to the Lesson

A leading Christian educator, Dr. Howard G. Hendricks, has described roles people play in a group situation. They fall into two categories and can be used in evaluating the members of any group.

Characteristics of Immaturity

The Onlooker—Content to be a silent spectator. Nods, smiles, and frowns. Other than this, he is a passenger instead of a crew member.

The Monopolizer—Brother Chatty. Rambles roughshod over the rest of the conversation with his verbal ability. Stubbornly clings to his right to say what he thinks—sometimes without thinking.

The Belittler—This is Mr. Gloom. He takes the dim view. Minimizes the contributions of others. Usually has three good reasons why "it will never work."

The Wisecracker—Feels called to a ministry of humor. Mr. Cheerio spends his time and talent as the group playboy. Indifferent to the subject at hand, he is always ready with the clever remark.

The Manipulator—Brother Ulterior knows the correct approach to the problem (obviously). He manipulates the proceedings so his plan will be adopted.

The Hitchhiker—Never had an original thought in his life. Unwilling to commit himself. Sits on the sidelines until the decision has jelled, then jumps on the bandwagon.

The Pleader—Chronically afflicted with obsessions. Always pleading for some cause or certain actions. Feels led to share this burden frequently. One-track mind.

The Sulker—Born in the objective case and lives in the kickative mood. The group won't accept his worthy contribution, so he sulks.

Characteristics of Maturity

The Proposer—Initiates ideas and action. Keeps things moving.

The Encourager—Brings others into the discussion. Encourages others to contribute. Emphasizes the value of their suggestions and comments. Stimulates others to greater activity by approval and recognition.

The Clarifier—The one who has the facility to step in when confusion, chaos, and conflict dominate. He defines the problem concisely. He points out the issues clearly.

The Analyzer—Examines the issues closely. Weighs the suggestions carefully. Never accepts anything without first "thinking it through."

The Explorer—Always moving into new and different areas. Probing relentlessly. Never satisfied with the obvious or the traditional.

The Mediator—Facilitates agreement or harmony between members, especially those who are making faces at each other. Seeks to find mediating solutions acceptable to all.

The Synthesizer—Is able to put the pieces together. Brings the different parts of the solution or plan together and synthesizes them.

The Programmer—The one who is ready with the ways and means to put the proposal into effect. Adept at organization. Moves in the realm of action. (Gleaned from *Lead Out, A Guide for Leading Bible Discussion Groups*, NavPress, Colorado Springs, Colorado, 1974, pages 6-61.)

It has been suggested in an earlier session that discipling is a both/and ministry. It is not one form in contrast to others, but a variety of ways of discipling another person. In the preceding session attention centered on the congregation of believers. This session will concentrate on the discipleship model in the context of small groups.

Goals for this session

1. You will understand the nature of small groups and how certain discipleship principles may be taught and learned in that context.

2. You will discover why some groups are effective and others are not, and to work toward an effective group.

3. You will learn some basic principles of group dynamics and group interaction.

4. You will know how to organize a discipleship group that will teach principles conducive to a group learning situation.

5. You will begin mentoring some fellow Christians in a group setting either for establishing or equipping.

As you begin...

Listen to the messages for Session Eleven (Cassette Tape 5)

The Lesson

The ministry and social activities of a balanced church can be characterized as large group, small group, and one-to-one ministry. The *large group* is the time of celebration when believers meet to gather together to worship God in spirit and truth.

The *small group* (or "cell group") usually has about 6 to 12 (maximum) people. This is where trust is developed, personal joys and problems are shared, and close friendships are built. These groups can take many forms. We can find Bible study groups, prayer groups, action groups, research groups, and many other kinds in and out of the church.

To these two activities might be added the *one-on-one* ministry of disciplemaking without taking away any of the programs already in operation in a given church. All these forms of church ministry mentioned above are biblical, for as we search the Scriptures, particularly the New Testament, we find clear examples of each one.

We want to examine the biblical foundation for small groups, then their nature, effectiveness, and dynamic, concluding with the place discipleship groups have in the church.

I. THE BIBLICAL FOUNDATION FOR SMALL GROUPS

There are times in the Bible when large numbers of people gather to worship or receive teaching, like the Hebrews at Mount Sinai receiving the Law (Exod. 19), the people of united Israel at the dedication of the Solomonic temple (1 Kings 8), or the crowds listening to Ezra preach the Word after the return from exile (Neh. 8:1-8). Examples in the New Testament are the feeding of the 5,000 and 4,000 in Jesus' ministry (Matt. 14:15-21; 15:29-39), or the preaching of Peter to the crowd in Jerusalem on the Day of Pentecost (Acts 2).

Most of the time, however, God's people gather in smaller groups, where there can be more intimacy and personal interaction. Fewer people together, too, simplifies management and leadership. We can see the wisdom of Jethro's advice to Moses to subdivide his judicial responsibilities under rulers of 1,000's, 100's, 50's, and 10's. We would do well, also, to heed his counsel.

A. Basic Unit of Community

The triune God, who lives eternally in communion of three Persons, created us to live in community. The most obvious expression of this principle is the family. God simply made it impossible to get into the human race without being part of a small loving fellowship. Not only was the marriage relationship the means of human reproduction, the home which it formed became the primary center of learning.

Small groups of mutual trust and love, when functioning as God intended, provide the most natural environment for discipleship. Leadership rests with the parents, of course, who are to teach the commandments of the Lord: "Impress them on your children. Talk about them when you sit at home and when you walk along the road, when you lie down and when you get up... Write them on the door frames of your houses and on your gates" (Deut. 6:7-9).

So from the beginning responsibility for religious education has resided in the home. That is why even in times of apostasy in Israel, when the kings and priests were utterly corrupt, the Word of God was not forgotten. There were faithful moms and dads who never bowed their house to Baal, and in the holy sanctuary of their homes, they taught their children to walk in the ways of the Lord.

Jesus brought this age-old principle into focus beautifully in his training of the twelve. He created a family of faith and learning, which only later came to be called the church.

The Holy Spirit guided the early church into following the same pattern set by Jesus. Believers met in small groups in houses, as there were no church buildings for nearly 200 years. We see Barnabas and Saul (later Paul) being sent out by a small group of five, then Paul duplicating that form throughout all of his ministry as his teams crisscrossed the Mediterranean world in small groups.

B. Building Up One Another

The constant call of Scripture is for Christians to build up fellow believers. God's Word is plain; in its most comprehensive form we are commanded to love one another as Christ loved us, or in John's words, "Whoever loves God must also love his brother" (1 John 4:21).

So many times in the New Testament we find expressions that call on Christians to be or to do something for "one another." We are to:

☑ *Love* one another (Rom. 13:8), for that is the fulfillment of the law of God.

☑ *Receive* one another (Rom. 15:7), that is, accept one another because Christ has received us; this brings God the glory he deserves.

☑ *Admonish* one another (Rom. 15:14), which is urging one another toward godly Christian behavior (see also Col. 3:16).

☑ *Care* for one another (1 Cor. 12:25), that is, look after one another's spiritual welfare (and physical if need be).

☑ *Bear* one another's burdens (Gal. 6:2); we are to help one another through the tough times and problems that come to us.

☑ *Belong* to one another as members of God's forever family. (Eph. 4:25)

☑ *Be kind* to one another, forgiving one another (Eph. 4:32).

☑ *Comfort* one another (1 Thess. 4:18) with the fact that Jesus is coming again.

☑ *Build up* one another (1 Thess. 5:11); this is the basic responsibility of all believers toward one another.

☑ *Pray* for one another (James 5:16), for that will have great positive results in the life of the one prayed for.

These one-another statements are a realistic description of the true Christian life and are often best expressed in the intimacy of a small group or cell.

The following cartoon communicates well the discipling concept of building one another up and sharing one another's burdens.

HOLDING UP ONE ANOTHER

II. THE NATURE OF SMALL GROUPS

Small groups give people the opportunity to get to know each other, to appreciate one another, to share burdens with one another, and do things together. They enable people to get out of the spectator mentality and become a participator with others in ministry.

People who have learned to love one another can grow together in the Lord. We are willing to learn from those whom we trust. The group dynamic allows greater learning to occur than listening to a lecture in a classroom setting. The very arrangement of a group in a relaxed setting, usually seated in a circle, makes one feel at home.

Such groups have many uses in the church. They can be used for Bible study, prayer, and discussion of vital issues having to do with living the Christian life. They can be action groups, involving training and strategizing outreach ministries. Small groups can also be used for support purposes, in which problems and difficulties are shared and healing of relationships takes place.

A healthy and long-lived group needs to have the following characteristics:

1. *A Common Sense of Purpose*—an acknowledged purpose and the means by which it will be achieved.

2. *Authority of Scripture*—only the Bible is recognized as authoritative, though each is encouraged to share opinions.

3. *A Commitment to Group Discipline*—these are the disciplines to which the group commits itself to accomplish its purpose.

4. *Mutual Accountability*—in all situations the group will learn to care for and challenge one another.

5. *Content of Faith*—consistent learning, growing in knowledge as well as grace.

6. *Honest Expression*—committed to sharing needs, hurts and joys.

7. *Confidentiality*—nothing shared in the group will be shared outside the group.

8. *Relevant Structure*—meetings are designed to meet the needs of the group.

9. *Prayer for one another*—each member covenants to pray for the others daily while the group meets.

10. *Centrality of Jesus Christ*—without Christ at the center of everything the group does, people can meet together but lives will not be transformed.

A discipling group exists to help persons mature in their walk with God, so they can be trained to minister to others.

REVIEW BEFORE YOU GO AHEAD

1. List three examples of small groups in biblical times.

_____

_____

_____

2. Why is the family so central in learning?

_____

_____

3. From the following list, check the "one another" statements in the New Testament that you need to work on at this time.

    ❏ Love one another   ❏ Receive one another
    ❏ Admonish one another   ❏ Care for one another
    ❏ Bear one another's burdens   ❏ Belong to one another
    ❏ Be kind to one another   ❏ Forgive one another
    ❏ Comfort one another   ❏ Build up one another
    ❏ Pray for one another

III. THE LEADERSHIP OF SMALL GROUPS

The effectiveness of a group rests largely upon its leaders. Where there is poor leadership, the group will have difficulty keeping alive. Yet almost anyone who is willing to learn can become a good leader with training and experience.

Here are twelve guidelines for leaders:

1. Set a tone of *friendliness*. Learn the names of everyone in the group. Greet them as a they arrive, and immediately make them feel comfortable. This requires that the leader always be there early.

2. Be *sensitive* to individual needs. Learn where the members of the group are coming from, where they are hurting, what problems they are facing in their lives.

3. *Share honestly* your own needs. The leader's transparency will create openness in the group. Refrain from confessing other people's sins, but do not hesitate to confess your own.

4. *Listen* with loving concern to what others are saying. Try to hear not only what they say, but what they feel. Keep eye contact with the group.

5. Keep the group's *purpose in focus*. Meetings can get off on tangents unless called back to their mission. If someone seems to sidetrack the group, you might say, "That's interesting, Bob, but let's look at this subject now." Or you could say, "We seem to be getting off the track," then move on.

6. *Ask questions* to direct thoughts. This is the way to keep the discussion on target without monopolizing the conversation. A good leader will talk no more than 20-30% of the time.

7. *Welcome silence*. Let people think. After asking a question, if no one responds in 60 seconds, you can ask, "Did everyone understand the question?", and then rephrase the question.

8. *Encourage participation*. If someone seems to dominate by talking too much, let the person finish, then say, "That's good. What does someone else think about it?" It is the responsibility of the leader to see that everyone takes part.

9. Get people to make *personal applications*. The leader must not let persons talk in generalities. Ask, "How is it at home, at school, at work?" You might say, "Give me a specific illustration of this in your own life, Bill." Ask them to use the first person singular — "I am facing..."

10. *Clarify* what is happening in the group. Help people see the issue. "What does this mean to you, Jane?" might be a question. Bring the discussion to a meaningful summary.

11. *Recognize* anger, conflict, boredom, and deal with it. "I see that this bothers you, Jim", you might say. "Would you like to tell us why?" Build bridges where there are barriers.

12. *Let the group minister to each other*. At this point the group really fulfills its purpose.

GROUP INACTION

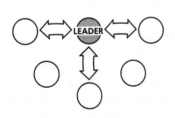

Wrong Way

GROUP INTERACTION

Right Way

IV. THE GROUP AS A DISCIPLING ENTITY

Everyone in a discipleship group should have the attitude of wanting to learn from others. The group, then, is an accountability session as well as a time of learning new facts, concepts, and ideas.

Here is a typical discipleship group meeting:

1. Time of Sharing (15-20 minutes)

During this period members of the group are free to talk about things that have been happening in their life since the last meeting. The leader may need to encourage someone to share. It is a time, too, when members can see how they are keeping the disciplines of the group. This may include a daily quiet time, Bible study, memorization of Scripture, witnessing assignments, fasting, or anything else agreed on by the group. In early stages this period should be longer in order to give persons more time to talk about their history.

2. Group Discussion (40-50 minutes)

In this period attention turns to the subject under study. It might be a Bible passage or a theme from Scripture, a doctrine, some life-centered question, like how to share your faith, or it could focus on a spiritual discipline, like prayer. Sometimes a devotional book or a Christian classic may be used as the reference. To bring this time to a close, the leader may summarize the main ideas that have come out in the discussion.

3. Prayer (15-20 minutes)

Requests can be shared by members of the group, including any personal needs. How you pray depends upon the group, but everyone should feel free to take part. Some times you will pray individually, and other times in unison; you may kneel, sit, stand, walk. All that matters is that you get through to God.

Before the meeting closes, the leader should make clear what the next meeting will cover, give any assignments, and make sure that everyone understands the time and place. Sometimes the group may want to linger for fellowship. Refreshments may be served, though not as a rule.

You see in this session the combining of teaching and training—group members are learning new biblical concepts through their study, and at the same time are being trained in the Christian disciplines.

These groups normally meet once a week for three months, concluding with an evaluation meeting. The group may decide to go on for another set period of time, perhaps with a different format and discipline. Some groups may want to terminate after a few months; others may continue for years. The important thing is to have regular check up periods to make sure that the group is fulfilling its purpose.

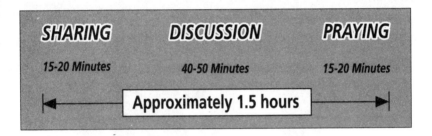

V. KINDS OF DISCIPLESHIP GROUPS

Different kinds of discipleship groups may be found in churches committed to the discipling ministry. One kind would be the type in which *training* of future disciplers takes place. The goal of this group is to enable each participant to start discipling another person. Since it began with committed *F-A-I-T-H* Christians who needed to learn the strategy of discipling, the group meetings simply provide the skills for doing so.

Another kind of discipleship group would be one in which the participants learn the basic *disciplines* of a walk with God. If desired, a number of in-depth materials have been developed by denominations and para-church organizations to assist groups in such a program.

A different kind of discipleship group would provide *support* for disciplers to keep them encouraged and motivated. In addition to sharing with one another from their Christian disciplines, this group would discuss problems encountered in their discipling and work on deepening of positive character qualities.

Some groups focus especially on *evangelism*, with their purpose centering on reaching people in the community with the Gospel. Meetings would give large place to acquiring new skills in witnessing, as well as prayer for one another and the churches' ministry of outreach. Many books and tapes by effective soul-winners are available to use as resources.

Still other discipleship groups exist primarily to **pray** for the work of God around the world. The agenda of these groups centers around Bible readings, reports from the mission field, prayer requests and seasons of earnest intercession.

There is no end to the variations of discipleship groups. Follow a pattern that best suits your need. If what has been done before does not satisfy, then try something else.

ALONE
- ☑ *No Belonging*
- ☑ *No Encouragement*
- ☑ *No Learning*
- ☑ *No Caring*

GROUP
- ☑ *Belonging*
- ☑ *Encouragement*
- ☑ *Learning*
- ☑ *Caring*

♦ *Ideas to remember*

This session has discussed the ministry of small groups in the local church, with particular reference to discipleship groups. The Bible and specifically Jesus' own ministry show the value and necessity of small groups in various ways operative in the church. The effectiveness of the early church was seen in their copying Jesus' methodology in what they did in the propagation of the Gospel in that first generation after Jesus ascended into heaven.

We then looked at the nature and effectiveness of a small group ministry in the church and emphasized the fact that this form of ministry was a *participatory* one (no spectators), which is the essence of the ministry committed by the Lord to all believers. It is a natural way to learn how to walk with God and how to reproduce the reality of that walk in the lives of others.

A brief discussion on the dynamic of small groups and their leadership followed, with the emphasis again placed on the discipleship type in the church. A suggested format for a discipleship meeting was given along with some variations of focus. In the whole session the emphasis again was on a both/and kind of ministry in the church — the traditional worship and educational meetings being supplemented by various kinds of small groups as well as continuing one-on-one relationships.

If the original Twelve, later grown to 120 in the Upper Room, could turn the Roman world topsy turvy with the Gospel in one generation, that methodology used today could do the same in our world of five billion plus.

Application of the Lesson

Here are some questions for reflection and application:

1. Check what kinds of small groups are presently active in your church.

   ❏ Prayer Group   ❏ Confirmation Class
   ❏ Discipleship Group   ❏ Support Group
   ❏ Bible Study Group   ❏ Ministry/Outreach Group
   ❏ Evangelistic Group   ❏ Sunday School Class
   ❏ Alcoholics Anonymous   ❏ Fellowship Group
   ❏ Community Action Group   ❏ _____

2. What kind or kinds of discipleship groups is your church ready for at this time? Why?

   _____

   _____

   _____

3. How would you go about implementing these groups?

   _____

   _____

   _____

4. Outline the kind of program you can use in your suggested discipleship group.

    _____

    _____

    _____

5. Memorize Galatians 6:2; Romans 13:8; 15:7 and James 5:16 in a Bible version of your choice.

SESSION 12
Living in Fulfillment of the Great Commission

Introduction to the lesson

Two men went into the hills above Los Angeles to pray, for they had read Jeremiah 33:3 and wanted to see the promises fulfilled before their eyes. God had said to his faithful prophet in prison, "Call to me, and I will answer you, and show you great and mighty things, which you do not know" (NKJV). How do you stake a claim on the promises of God? The two wanted to know, so they covenanted with each other to pray together every morning until they felt assured that God was going to fulfill that promise in their lives.

Every morning at 5:00 AM they were up in the hills, kneeling with open Bibles before them, praying by name for the boys God had given them through their Sunday school and Boys' Club ministry. Each weekday they prayed for two hours, then headed down again to be at work by 8:00 AM. On Sundays they prayed for three hours before going to church.

As the days passed, they began praying for Harbor City, Torrance, Long Beach, Los Angeles, Pasadena, then the surrounding cities. In the third week they began extending their prayer interests up the West Coast—San Francisco, Oakland, Portland, Seattle. As they prayed, they soaked up the promises of God, and he gave them the faith to believe that they could be used to reach men for Christ from all 48 states. So they began praying, "Lord, use us to reach men from Oregon, Texas, Illinois, and Florida," mentioning every state then part of the union.

As their vision and faith grew, they bought a map of the world, putting their fingers on China, Japan, Formosa, Cyprus, France, Kenya, Venezuela, pleading with God for men in these far off places,

"Lord, allow us to serve you some day in each of these places and enable us to reach men for you in every one of these continents of the world." After 42 days they felt the burden lift, and they began to thank God that he had heard them and was going to fulfill what he had promised.

By the time World War II began (December 1941) Dawson Trotman discovered that in his work with sailors from the Pacific Fleet, men from every one of the 48 states had been touched by his ministry and had visited his home. Jeremiah 33:3 had been partially fulfilled. By the time that war ended four years later, the men he had led to Christ touched other lives on all the continents of the world, including most of the countries for which he had so earnestly prayed.

By the time he died only 11 years later, Jeremiah 33:3 had been completely fulfilled for him in his ministry. That 42-day prayer meeting, he wrote later, "was the turning point in my life." From that time on he lived out the Great Commission as a lifestyle. Though being dead, he still speaks, for his life and ministry serve as an ongoing example of commitment to men and women who would follow in his steps. (Adapted and abridged from *The Navigator* by Robert D. Foster, NavPress, pages 42-46.)

The call of Scripture always has been a call to commitment in the totality of life; those who would follow Jesus as his disciples must not only walk with him, their whole lifestyle must demonstrate the Great Commission visibly before the watching world. May God in his grace enable all of us—the writers, the editors, the readers, the students, and the mentors of this self-study course to live in fulfillment of the Great Commission.

Goals for this session

1. You will commit yourself personally to a lifestyle of discipleship to the glory of God.
2. You will promote the discipleship model of life and ministry in your church, denomination, and Christian friends.
3. You will pledge (to the Lord) to make any necessary changes in your life to live that way visibly.
4. You will develop a vision for the world that God has on his heart by doing everything you can to help fulfill the Great Commission.
5. You will live out that vision practically by becoming a spiritual reproducer of discipleship principles in the lives of others.

As you begin...

Listen to the messages for Session Twelve (Cassette Tape 5)

The Lesson

As we have said from the beginning, if we are going to be *disciplemakers*, we first have to be *disciples*. That is a prerequisite that cannot be violated. Only disciples make disciples, so we have to practice a regular walk with God before we can teach and train someone else to walk with God. And one of the ingredients of discipleship is to work toward fulfilling the Great Commission. This means that we have to appropriate the power of God through the indwelling Holy Spirit to live that kind of lifestyle and victorious life.

What, then, we might ask, is the motivation for that kind of changed lifestyle? The biblical answer is to have the heart and mind of God in our hearts and minds; that is called *world vision* — seeing our world through God's eyes, hearing the cry of needy humans through God's ears, meeting the needs of humanity with God's solution. Vision is not something that suddenly comes to us; it must be developed. And vision also is not something that can be taught; it must be caught. Then, when it is caught, our lives must live it out consciously and visibly to the end of our days.

Not only must we live our daily lives in light of the vision we have caught from God, but we must as best we can transmit it to others, so that future generations till Jesus comes again might know, live, practice, and transmit that vision. That, of course, is the essence of spiritual reproduction. When we are living our lives God's way and seeing everything through his eyes, we pass that on to another person in such a way that he or she will continue the process and transmit that lifestyle and vision to others who will do the same to others.

The closing challenge of this self-study course is for us to commit ourselves to living the rest of our lives in fulfillment of the Great Commission.

I. THE GREAT COMMISSION LIFESTYLE

The Great Commission lifestyle is living the totality of our daily lives in light of our responsibility to make disciples of all peoples of the world. Even though our own personal ministries may be restricted to a small area in one city of one country in this world, we can have the vision of the Gospel going out to all nations as we carry out the mission in our location.

Men and women whom God has used across the centuries have always been "both/and" people. For that is the essence of the final words of Jesus: "You will receive power, when the Holy Spirit comes upon you, and you will be my witnesses *both* in Jerusalem *and* in all Judea *and* in Samaria *and* to the remotest end of the earth" (Acts 1:8, BERK, emphasis added). The original Greek uses a particle with the two "and's" to show that the action spoken of is to be done in *all* those places.

J. B. Phillips has brought out this rendering very nicely in his paraphrase: "You are to be given power when the Holy Spirit has come to you. You will be witnesses to me, not only in Jerusalem, not only throughout Judea, not only in Samaria, but to the very ends of the earth." Christians are to do their ministry where they are located, but at the same time they should have an interest in and an involvement in what is going on elsewhere in the world— through prayer, giving, and perhaps going when the opportunity presents itself.

The Great Commission lifestyle, then, is living and breathing God's mission. It is the commitment we make to be knowledgeable about and involved in that mission in every way possible. It is the sincere prayer we pray daily: "Lord, use me *anyway–anytime– anywhere*!" Then by faith we expect God to answer that prayer with surprising opportunities that will affect others worldwide. The Great Commission lifestyle is developing a vision for God's world and doing something actively about making Christ known everywhere we can and training others to do the same. It is a way of life in which we expect our spiritual disciplines to prepare us for anything that may come along that day. In order to develop a lifestyle of that quality we have to be men and women of the Word and prayer, we have to be disciples of Jesus in the full meaning of that term (committed learners and followers of Christ), and we have to get to know more of what is happening in our world.

The Great Commission lifestyle includes quality times of prayer alone and with a group, interceding with the Lord for specific missionary activities worldwide. Through our prayers we get to have a part in the progress of the Gospel in far off places, laboring invisibly side by side with our missionaries and nationals of other countries.

The Great Commission lifestyle involves us with people with whom we come in contact daily, and makes us sensitive to their needs. Each day we pray for opportunities to share the Gospel, then discover that God gives us many occasions to so do.

The closer we draw to the Lord, the more we will know what is on his heart and mind. The more we know what is on his heart and mind, the more we will want to do what he wants done with our lives. We discover that the will of God is good, well-pleasing, and perfect (see Romans 12:2).

II. CHANGES REQUIRED IN OUR OWN LIVES

The closer we come to Jesus, the more we will discover in our lives what needs to be purged and what needs to be put in. The more we study God's Word to discover his will, the more we will find that will and have to make changes in our daily habit patterns and activities. We must die to self. The cross of Christ allows no compromise with carnality or self-centeredness.

Change requires effort, and the transition from self to servanthood may be painful. It starts in our basic attitudes, then affects our plans and our actions. Paul has summarized this self-giving lifestyle with these words: "For we do not preach ourselves, but Christ Jesus as Lord, and ourselves as your servants for Jesus' sake" (2 Cor. 4:5). That means we have to change from what we normally are to being servants of all with whom we come in contact.

To summarize:
- We serve God by serving people.

- We serve our fellow believers in Christ by encouraging them and building them up in the faith.

- We serve non-Christians by bringing the Gospel to them.

- We serve our enemies by loving them in Christ and praying for them.

- We serve ourselves by being servants to others, for the greatest satisfaction in life comes from having served.

To be servants of God and servants of others we have to set aside our inherent selfishness to be cleansed from sin. We cannot make this change in our own strength, but must depend wholly on the grace of God and the power of the indwelling Holy Spirit to bring it to pass. The Great Commission lifestyle is the life and ministry of servanthood.

Serving Others

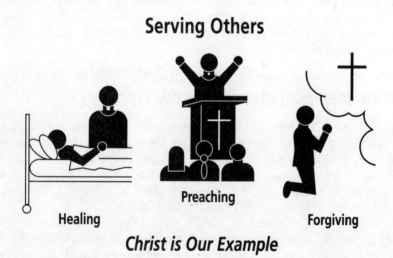

Healing

Preaching

Forgiving

Christ is Our Example

REVIEW BEFORE YOU GO AHEAD

1. Define the Great Commission lifestyle.

_____

_____

_____

2. Why is change necessary to develop the Great Commission lifestyle?

_____

_____

_____

3. What changes in your own life do you need to make as a result of this study?

_____

_____

_____

III. DEVELOPING WORLD VISION

A good rendering of Proverbs 29:18 reads: "Where there is no revelation [prophetic vision], the people cast off restraint; but happy is he who keeps the law" (NKJV). Where the Word of God is not proclaimed, people live any way they want to live, but the person who lives by the Bible has an enjoyable life.

An example of how Jesus developed world vision in his disciples can be seen in the incident with the woman at the well in Samaria (John 4:1-42). Here while Jesus talks with the woman about her need, the disciples were concerned about filling their stomachs with food. When they realize that Jesus had not eaten, it gave him a wonderful opportunity to explain that his food was doing the will of

God. Then, making an analogy to the disciples' need for a world vision, he said: "Do you not say, 'There are still four months and then comes the harvest'? Behold, I say to you, lift up your eyes and look at the fields, for they are already white for harvest!" (verse 35, NKJV).

The words "look at" do not mean just taking a casual glance, but to gaze intently at something; in the New Testament this term has in it the idea of having a careful and deliberate vision that interprets its object. Thus *gazing intently* at the fields of humankind will enable us to see the spiritual harvest that is ready there for a Gospel presentation. World vision is seeing that harvest through the eyes of God, then falling in step with his plan for our lives to be harvest workers in those fields.

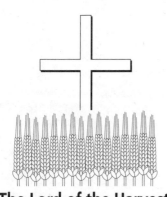

The Lord of the Harvest

This vision will focus the imperative of multiplying disciples who can show the love of Christ to a lost world. "When [Jesus] saw the multitudes, he was moved with compassion for them, because they were weary and scattered, like sheep having no shepherd. Then he said to his disciples, 'The harvest truly is plentiful, but the laborers are few. Therefore pray the Lord of the harvest to send out laborers into his harvest'" (Matt. 9:36-38, NKJV). So the disciples started praying and before long Jesus sent them out as the answers to their own prayers, "These twelve Jesus sent out" (Matt. 10:5).

IV. PRACTICAL DAILY LIVING IN LIGHT OF THAT VISION

What, then, is involved in our receiving, developing, maintaining, and growing in our vision? As has already been mentioned, it includes getting to know God's Word by all means available to us—hearing, reading, studying, memorizing, meditating on, and applying its truths to life. It means spending quality time in the presence of the Lord in our devotional times and speaking with him in meaningful prayer. The process may be summarized in the following ways.

1. Vision involves *knowing the person of God*. Paul's great desire and passion in his mature years was verbalized in this way: "[I want to] know him [Jesus] and the power of his resurrection, and the fellowship of his sufferings, being conformed to his death" (Phil. 3:10, NKJV). The only way we can do this is to spend personal time with him in the Word and in prayer.

2. Vision involves *compassion for people whom God loves*. The world of men and women whom God created in his own image and likeness is very much on his heart and is the very essence of John 3:16. A short journey through the Gospel of John will show the many references to the concern Jesus had for people.

3. Vision embodies *concern for places in the world*. We find mention in the Scriptures of strategic places, both positive and negative. The Great Commission is verbalized in terms of geographical areas (Acts 1:8). The mention of so many places is but a reflection of the fact that many people live in these places, thus vision involves having the perspective of God with respect to people and places, today particularly the great cities of the world.

4. Vision leads to *specific plans* to reach the world with the Gospel of Christ. When we start getting on our hearts the heart and mind of God, we get a glimpse into the plan he has for reaching our world with the Gospel in our generation. So we commit ourselves to follow his plan and do things his way.

5. Vision finds expression in *persons we are seeking to disciple*, men and women who will become workers in God's harvest. These committed disciplemakers are God's method in reaching the world.

6. Vision involves *prayer, much prayer*. We pray for people in need, but especially for those select few God has led into our lives to disciple. Here our faith can lay hold upon all the resources of God. That is why it can be said that ultimately our work is more a ministry of prayer than anything else.

7. Vision includes *practical actions*. We cannot much pray for God's will to be done without committing ourselves to do all we can to fulfill the request. Finally, then, through the power of the Spirit of Christ, we *do* the vision.

REVIEW BEFORE YOU GO AHEAD

1. Define world vision in your own words.

_____

_____

_____

2. What did Jesus try to teach his disciples at the well of Sychar in Samaria?

_____

_____

_____

3. What are some practical ways of developing world vision?

_____

_____

_____

4. What vision for ministry (serving others) do you believe God has for you?

V. TRANSMITTING THE VISION

The Great Commission lifestyle must be reproduced in the lives of others. Our discipling responsibilities in establishing and equipping younger Christians includes transmitting that vision to our trainees. This will include teaching the practical suggestions in the section above, as well as talking about the world God loves as a means of our trainees *catching* the vision from us.

While teaching our trainees to share their faith we must help them catch and then develop a God-given vision for the world. It is our responsibility as disciplers to make sure that our trainees become world Christians and are able to reproduce that vision eventually in the lives of others.

OVERVIEW OF DISCIPLEMAKING MINISTRY: CYCLE OF REPRODUCTION

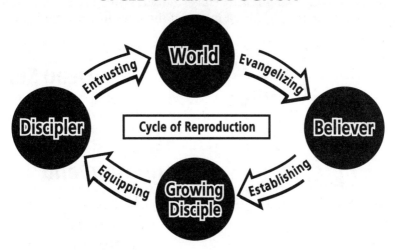

♦ *Ideas to remember*

This course has emphasized from beginning to end that Christ's mandate to make disciples of all nations is a command. It is not a mere call to full-time service, nor is it some special gift of the Spirit. The Great Commission is a life-style; it is the way Christ directed his steps while he lived among us on this earth, and now the way that he asks his disciples to follow.

Of course, it takes a disciple to make a disciple. If we are going to be used in discipling others in the Great Commission life-style, we first must be sure that we are walking with God and practicing basic disciplines of a holy life.

Included in these Christian disciplines is telling others about Jesus Christ. This means that the total lifestyle of one of Jesus' disciples must involve not only "intake" through the Spirit and the Word but also "output" through Christian ministry.

Have you ever heard anyone discuss the difference between the Sea of Galilee and the Dead Sea? Both have an intake of pure water. The difference is that the Dead Sea has no outlet. The water stalls within the lake and grows stagnant and stale. Some Christians' lives are like that. Their problem is not intake, but output—they are taking in good spiritual food, but with no outlet their lives are growing stale and stagnant. A consistent lifestyle of reaching out to others with the love of Christ is one of the keys to spiritual health.

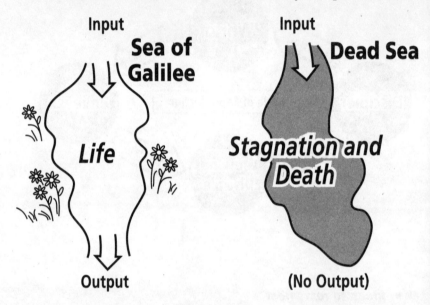

When we follow the teachings and example of Jesus and those of the early church, we are practicing the Great Commission lifestyle. This lifestyle includes catching and practicing world vision, then committing ourselves to be what God wants us to be and do what he wants us to do ...anyway ...anytime ...anywhere! This will mean making conscious changes in our lives to conform more and more to what we should be according to the Word of God.

We develop world vision by getting to know our Lord so well through the intake of Scripture and prayer that what is on his heart and mind becomes what is on our hearts and minds as well. We practice living the Great Commission lifestyle daily growing in our faith and in our participation in reaching this world with the gospel. One of the ways we do that is to transmit to other faithful men and women the vision we have received from God.

The tape *"Born to Reproduce"* which you have heard describes this kind of life. The thesis is very simple: People are born again by the Spirit of God in this world in order to reproduce spiritually. The analogy of human reproduction is based on God's command, "Be fruitful and multiply," given to Adam and to Noah. Christians are to be fruitful and multiply spiritually, for we have been born (spiritually) to reproduce.

Where this is not happening, we must find out why and deal with the problem. Every Christian has the potential to become a reproducer. It can be learned, but it takes time both to reach maturity ourselves, then patiently work with other persons to lead them to Christ and to maturity.

Would it be fair to ask: "Where is your man? Where is your woman? Where is the person you have led to Jesus and are now discipling? Is that person now reproducing for Christ?" May God enable you to be a spiritual reproducer to many generations!

Application of the Lesson

Here are some questions for reflection and application:

1. What specific plans do you have for participating in the vision God has for his world?

   _____

   _____

   _____

2. How are the persons with whom you are working right now beginning to reproduce the Great Commission vision in others?

   _____

   _____

   _____

3. Note how you continue to keep in touch with persons with whom you have invested your life:
   - ❏ Prayer
   - ❏ Sending tapes/books
   - ❏ Messages through others
   - ❏ Telephone calls
   - ❏ Shared ministry
   - ❏ _____
   - ❏ Occasional recreation times
   - ❏ Letters
   - ❏ Faxes
   - ❏ Periodic reunions
   - ❏ Visits

4. How do your prayers reflect your vision of the Great Commission?

   _____

   _____

   _____

   _____

5. Memorize 2 Cor. 4:5; John 17:25, 26; and Phil. 2:6-11 in a Bible version of your choice. Then review all the Bible verses you have memorized in this course.

Final Mentor Review

Make arrangements for your final review with your Mentor, reporting what you have been learning in this course. Discuss with your mentor how far you have led your trainee toward maturity. Has this person been able to communicate a vision to the younger Christian he or she has been helping to follow-up? In other words, have you been able to see the multiplication process begin?

Be sure that both you and your mentor understand how the course requirements are to be fulfilled so that you can be accorded the proper credit and certificate.

SESSION 13
Course Review

Introduction to the lesson

Mother Theresa of Calcutta, India, has achieved world renown not because she is such an eloquent *speaker* on the needs of the poor around the world, but because for the many years of her adult life she has been a practitioner of actually ministering self-sacrificially to the poor in a city of great need.

She has taught countless people what it means to bring a cup of water in the name of Jesus to one who is thirsty (Matt. 25:33-40). But then that has always been the teaching of Scripture, perhaps best expressed by James, when he said:

> *"But prove yourselves doers of the word, and not merely hearers who delude themselves" (James 1:22, NASB).*

This grand statement on "practicing what we preach or teach" is then followed by the illustration of a person looking in a mirror and not doing what the glass reveals must be done (James 1:23-25). Jesus reserved his harshest language and warning for those who did not do what they said they believed or taught. Hypocrisy always has been a temptation among Christians and churches.

This lesson has been designed as a summary for all the other lessons in this self-study course. It also serves as the final checkup on our *practicing* what we have learned, so we can impart effectively these biblical truths to others whom we might be discipling.

Goals for this session

1. You will review the entire content of this course unit by unit.

2. You will check up on yourself to see if you have applied the needed biblical truths to your own life before attempting to teach them to others.

3. You will reconfirm your commitment to Jesus as the Lord of your life and ministry.

4. You will rededicate yourself to making disciples of all nations by following Jesus' vision and pattern to reach this world with the Gospel.

5. You will set realistic goals for reaching people with the Gospel, then following them up and discipling them for the glory of God.

The Lesson

For a rapid review of the teaching content of this course, you may want to page through each of the twelve sessions, unit by unit, and read the answers you wrote in the brief reviews inserted throughout the lessons. This should refresh your memory about the basic ideas that were emphasized, and will give you an overview of the entire curriculum.

I. LAYING THE FOUNDATIONS

The first unit laid the foundation for the ministry of follow-up and disciplemaking by confronting us with the person of God in his trinitarian revelation—Father, Son, and Holy Spirit.

The response God calls from those of us who have become Christians or his people (Old Testament) by grace through faith is that we walk with him in newness of life. That call to walking with God is a call to every single believer without exception. When we do that, we then realize that we are people with a mission, and we share our faith and walk with others, carrying out God's mission to the end of our days or until Jesus comes again.

When we look at Jesus in the Gospels and the rest of the New Testament, we find him to be the One who confirms God's plan by carrying it out in history. He secured our salvation and taught us how to live and minister most effectively. Then in appropriating the power of the blessed Holy Spirit and in obedience to the Great Commission of Jesus we live our lives and make disciples of others. This sets us in the great sweep of other brothers and sisters who have believed in Christ, lived for him, and served him loyally throughout history.

Review Application Statements

As you consider this foundation in the work and teaching of the Holy Trinity, test yourself through these statements:

- ☑ I believe in and have received Jesus Christ as my Lord and Savior.

- ☑ I have committed myself to walking with God lovingly and willingly in all of life (review F-L-O-C-K-S).

- ☑ On the basis of my walk with God I am making a deliberate effort to be a witness for Jesus Christ.

- ☑ I am willing to be taught and trained by Jesus through Scripture.

- ☑ I understand and am committed to follow Jesus' pattern of ministry.

- ☑ I am trusting in God's grace and the power of the Holy Spirit to enable me to carry out my ministry according to Jesus' pattern.

- ☑ I am committed to being in step with the movements of revival in my area of ministry today.

II. ESTABLISHING NEW BELIEVERS

The second unit of this course introduced you to the whole process of following up new believers, then beginning to disciple them toward maturity and spiritual reproduction. The whole process was then illustrated in a series of diagrams in a number of subsequent chapters as follows (verbal summary):

- ♦ We *Evangelize* the WORLD.

- ♦ We *Establish* the [NEW] BELIEVER.

- ♦ We *Equip* GROWING DISCIPLES.

- ♦ We *Entrust* DISCIPLERS with the responsibility of *repeating* the process.

Session 4 discussed the reasons for follow-up and its process; then it surveyed some of the goals and objectives of follow-up, and concluded with biblical principles of how we can help new Christians grow in their faith ("spiritual pediatrics").

The practical ways of following up a new believer were discussed in Session 5, with a stress on the beginning disciplines of a daily quiet time, Scripture memory, sermon notetaking, and training for witness within the context of the local church. Included in this study were the qualifications of a discipler and two key illustrations — the Word Hand and the Prayer Hand.

After the new believer has begun growing through the disciplines introduced above, then the process changes from "immediate follow-up" to either "advanced follow-up" or "basic discipling." This discussion in Session 6 included seeing the whole picture through The Navigators' "Wheel Illustration," the introduction of two more basic "Word Hand" disciplines, learning a Gospel presentation, and full association with or joining a local church and participating fully in its threefold ministry.

Further Review Application Statements

Test yourself on the following statements as giving account to the Lord:

- ☑ I understand the reasons for and the process of follow-up.

- ☑ I have begun actually following up a new believer.

- ☑ I know what the goals and objectives of follow-up are, as well as its biblical principles.

- ☑ I understand the Word Hand and Prayer Hand illustrations, and am by God's grace practicing their teachings.

- ☑ I am a member of a local church and am involved in its life and ministry, including witnessing regularly.

- ☑ I am growing in Bible study and meditation on God's Word, knowing a gospel presentation, and in all the aspects of my being a member of a local church.

III. EQUIPPING GROWING BELIEVERS

Establishing new believers eventually produces a growing disciple. This is a person who is now progressing steadily in his or her commitment to the lordship of Christ and to the spiritual disciplines.

The need now is to be equipped for ministry (see Eph. 4:11-12), and that process is discussed in this unit. Reread these chapters, and review your knowledge and commitments.

Through the teaching/training process the discipler by example conveys to the willing trainee some strong character qualities of discipleship. By this stage of growth the trainee has become a *F-A-I-T-H* Christian and is ready to build vision, knowledge, and skills into his or her life. Session 7 suggests a strategy for this stage of the discipling process, some of the qualities to be worked on, and the accountability procedures in the church.

A major ingredient in the equipping process is the ministry of sharing one's faith. Since this spiritual ministry is the responsibility of every believer, the growing disciple needs to learn how to do so effectively and with the assistance of the discipler to develop strategies for witness and evangelism individually and through the local church. Session 8 teaches how to give an effective Gospel witness.

The second stage of the equipping process is to bring the trainee to the place where he or she becomes a discipler by the grace of God. Session 9 discusses the overall objectives of the disciplemaking ministry, pointing out the basic characteristics of the person ready to become a discipler. Some practical strategies for selection and training in spiritual multiplication and infiltration were given, with suggestions for one-on-one and group meetings, as well as being part of a ministry team.

Additional Review Application Statements

Here is another set of accountability statements that you should test yourself by in order to be an effective discipler:

- ☑ I understand the equipping process in disciplemaking, and am putting it into practice with my trainee.

- ☑ By God's grace and empowering I am a F-A-I-T-H Christian and so is my God-given trainee.

- ☑ I am accountable to Christ and to my church for my own life and for the progress with my trainee.

- ☑ I am regularly sharing a word of truth and my personal testimony, and teaching my trainee to do the same.

- ☑ I know how to present the Gospel and do so with my trainee.

☑ I understand that the eventual goal of the discipling process is to have my trainee become a discipler, and am working with him or her to that end.

☑ I am practicing the principles of multiplication and infiltration, and am involved with my trainee in one-on-one time, group meetings, and ministry with a church team.

IV. DEVELOPING A DISCIPLING CHURCH

Since we as believers are not called to function and minister alone, we must share our vision for follow-up and disciplemaking with the body of which we are a part. Thus a disciplemaker should pray and work to make his or her local fellowship of believers a disciplemaking church.

If you are a pastor, you should try by God's grace to pass on what you have been learning to your board and your people; if you serve on the governing board of your church, then you must share what you have learned with them and with your pastor or pastoral staff. If you are not an officer in your church, than again through prayer and example you should try to get your church to catch the vision of spiritual reproduction.

Since the most comprehensive picture the New Testament gives us of the church is that of "the body of Christ," it is obvious that every part of the body must do its part if that entity is to be healthy and functioning. The Holy Spirit of God has provided spiritual gifts to every member of that body for this purpose. Specific suggestions are given in Session 10 on how your church might integrate the discipleship model into its life and ministry.

It has been demonstrated that churches function best when some form of small group life and opportunity exists in its life and ministry. In the New Testament letters we find a whole series of admonitions that use the expression "one another," suggesting various ministries we are to have to each other. Session 11 notes the nature and leadership of small groups, as well as some practical suggestions for discipleship group activities.

What ties the whole course together is catching the vision for this kind of ministry through our consistent walk with God and service for him. The call of God to his disciples is that we live and practice a Great Commission lifestyle, having on our hearts clearly what God has on his—the carrying out of his mission to the ends of the earth (see Matthew 24:14). Session 12 teaches what that lifestyle means and emphasizes how we can develop world vision and how we can transmit that vision to our trainees, the men and women whom we are discipling.

The Final Set of Review Application Statements

Here are some final statements against which you should test your life and ministry if you are to profit most from this course:

- ☑ I am committed to my church, to its life and ministry, and to its God-given leadership structure.

- ☑ I have discovered, developed, and am using my spiritual gift or gifts.

- ☑ With God's help and as I am able I will take part in helping my congregation integrate the discipleship model into its life and ministry.

- ☑ I understand the need for small group ministries in my church, and will do my part in helping them start or develop in my church as I am able.

- ☑ I am asking the Lord to deepen his vision for this world in my life so that I can assist someone else in "catching that vision."

- ☑ By God's grace I am committed to live my whole life as a servant of Jesus Christ according to the Great Commission lifestyle.

♦ Closing Exhortation

This course was written with you in mind, you who want to live as a disciple of Jesus Christ and make other disciples. You have seen that disciplemaking has been God's plan from the beginning. Supremely, our Lord modelled and taught this approach to ministry. You have gained new insight and learned many practical ways to help other believers to grow.

But the bottom line is your own life. *Disciplemaking begins with you.* You have to be a disciple before you can make a disciple. You need to commit yourself to a lifetime of walking with Christ, a commitment that must be renewed each day. You need to make John the Baptist's testimony your own: "He [Jesus] must increase, but I must decrease" (John 3:30, NASB).

As you follow Christ wholeheartedly, others will be drawn to your life. Your own commitment will provide a platform for ministering to others. Like Christ, you must take on the role of a servant and meet other's needs.

But not in your own strength! The Holy Spirit desires to fill you and empower you for ministry. Never forget that Paul concluded his great declaration about his commitment to discipleship (Col. 1:28) by affirming in verse 29: "To this end I labor, struggling with all *his* energy, which so powerfully works in me." Making disciples at times will be a struggle; but God's power is sufficient for our every need!

Will you commit yourself to the Great Commission Lifestyle? If the following prayer expresses the desire of your heart, pray it with sincerity right now:

> *Lord, in humble dependence upon you and your strength, I desire that you use my life anyway, anytime, anywhere. May your fervent desire to make disciples become the consuming passion of my life.*

It is a prayer God will delight to answer.

$\mathcal{F}$ORMS

☑ Student and Mentor Agreement

☑ Mentor Final Review

Instructions

As you begin this course, select a mentor and complete the Student and Mentor Agreement. Then mail it to the *Institute of Evangelism, Billy Graham Center, Wheaton, IL, 60187, U.S.A.* This will place you on record as a student in this course.

As instructed in the manual, meet occasionally with your mentor. He or she will monitor your progress through the material. When you have completed the entire course, then your mentor should complete the Mentor Final Review Form and send it to the Institute of Evangelism. It is the responsibility of the mentor to confirm that you have completed the course requirements.

After the Institute of Evangelism has received the Student and Mentor Agreement and the Mentor Final Review Form, you will receive a certificate recognizing your efforts in studying this course. It is your responsibility to see that these forms are properly completed. If the Institute does not receive your forms or they are illegible or incomplete, you may not receive a certificate of accomplishment.

Student and Mentor Agreement

For my study of the *Follow-up and Disciplemaking* course, I have chosen

(print name) _____

to be my Mentor, whose signature below indicates acceptance of that role and its responsibilities. We have agreed to meet according to the recommended schedule (every three weeks). My completion of study, and of the course assignments, is tentatively set within six months after my enrollment date.

Student's Signature _____

Student's Name (print) _____

Mailing Address _____

_____

Enrollment Date _____

Completion Date (proposed) _____

I have read the requirements for satisfactory completion of the Billy Graham Center extension course in *Disciplemaking*, and I will periodically check the progress of the student named above. When course study is completed, I will prepare the Mentor Final Review (IOE Form 92-2), for prompt filing with the Billy Graham Center.

Mentor's Signature: _____

Title: _____

Church or Organization: _____

Relationship to student (*Circle one*):

Spouse Teacher Pastor Friend Other _____

Mentor Final Review

Student's Name: _____

(Print name plainly as it is to appear on Certificate)

The student named above has faithfully and conscientiously studied the Billy Graham Center extension course titled *Follow-up and Disciplemaking*, complete all written exercises and consulting with me periodically to review progress. I judge the student's acquaintance with the instructional materials to be:

_____ Superior _____ Average _____ Acceptable

I believe this student has benefited most from the course in regard to:

_____

_____

_____

I recommend further study in the following area(s):

_____

_____

_____

I congratulate the student for special excellence in the areas of:

_____

_____

_____

I hereby endorse this student for certification.
(Mentor's signature)

_____

$\mathcal{A}$PPENDICES

A. Quiet Time

B. Scripture Memory

C. Knowing God

D. The Bridge Illustration

E. Transcription for Dawson Trotman

F. Selected Bibliography

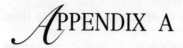PPENDIX A

Quiet Time

*"I love the Lord because He hears my prayers
and answers them. Because He bends down and
listens, I will pray as long as I breathe!"*
(Psalm 116:1, 2 Living Bible)

TIME ALONE WITH GOD

Did you know that God wants to spend time alone with you?[1]
That thought may amaze you...but consider it for a moment:

When a person accepts Jesus Christ as Lord and Savior, he
becomes a member of God's family...a child of God[2] ...he can call God
his father![3] Any good father wants to spend time with his children —
sometimes with all of them together...but often with each one alone.
That is the way that a person gets to know another person well — by
spending time alone with him.

So the best way to get to know your Heavenly Father is to spend
time alone with Him. There's nothing mystical about it. He has made
it clear that He is interested in us who are His children.[4]

The simple and yet marvelous way in which we can get to know
God better through spending time alone with Him is by reading His
Word and conversing with Him in prayer.

Of course we can pray to Him any time of the day — driving to
work, mixing a cake, washing clothes, studying at school — but
really to spend time alone with someone is to give attention to him
without distractions.

Perhaps the morning is best for you...when you're fresh, before
your active day begins. Or perhaps the evening is the best time for
you to spend time with God...at the close of your day, as you prepare
for the rest He offers.

Whatever the time, be consistent in meeting Him. Jesus rose
early to pray...and He went somewhere that was quiet[5] — a good
idea for us!

There is no ritual to your time alone with God...any more than there would be in spending time alone with an earthly parent.

A word of greeting should come first...a short prayer to God asking His blessing on your time together.[6]

Then you'll want to read something of His Word to you.[7] You will likely find the Gospel of John the most interesting if you are just getting acquainted with the Bible, for it is here that God's plan for you through Jesus Christ is most beautifully summed up in one book.[8]

After you have finished reading John, you may wish to continue in the Book of Acts to see how the early Christians shared their faith with those around them. Sharing your faith is one of the most important things you can do for God.

If you have not read much from the Bible, you may prefer to use a modern version rather than the regular King James version. The New Testament was written originally in common, not classical, Greek so that people could understand its important message.

While you are reading, meditate. To meditate simply means to think seriously about spiritual things. To meditate on what you are reading is to think quietly, soberly, and deeply about God — how wonderful He is, what wonderful things He has done for you, what He is going to do for you, what He wants you to do.[9] Perhaps you will notice:

♦ a special promise for you to claim

♦ a guidepost to help you in your daily life

♦ a command you should follow

♦ a searchlight that is pointing out some sin in your life[10]

♦ a meaningful verse you will want to memorize

Don't read too fast or try to finish too much at one time. Take time to look for all that God has for you in the portion you do read. You don't need to rush through your time alone with God, especially if you spend some time with Him each day.

When you've read and meditated a while, then converse with God in prayer. Talk to Him as you would to your own earthly parent who loves you, who wants the best for you, who wants to help you in every way possible.

Perhaps you don't know what to talk over with God in prayer. These few suggestions may help you:

You can *praise* Him for what He is...Creator and Sustainer of the entire universe[11] ...yet interested in each of us who are His family!

You can *thank* Him for all He has done...for all He is doing for you...and for all He will do for you.[12]

You can tell Him about the things you have done and said and thought for which you are sorry...this is *confessing* your sins. He tells us in His Word that He is able and faithful to forgive our sins.[13]

You can pray for your *family*...we have special obligation for our own.

You can pray for *others*[14] ...for friends or neighbors who have needs, physical or spiritual. You can ask God to work in the heart of some person you hope will come to know Christ as Savior...even as you have done. Remember those who are new Christians. You can also pray for our government officials, for your minister and church officers, for missionaries and other Christian servants.

You can pray for *yourself*[15] ...ask His guidance for the new day[16] ...ask Him to help you with problems you have[17] ...ask Him to help you do His will for the day...ask Him to arrange opportunities to serve Him through helping others by means of words and works.

You may want to list your prayer requests, so you don't forget any, and so you can record God's answers... "yes," or "no," or "wait."[18] Use a small notebook or note cards.

If you have spent your time alone with God in the morning, then continue your day, refreshed and ready for what may come your way!

If you have spent your time alone with Him in the evening, then go to sleep relaxed in His care, ready to rest for a new day of service to Him.

You may find it possible to spend some time alone with God both morning and evening.

Be sure to remember that you can pray to Him any time, anywhere...in school, at work, at home...about anything...to ask for something that is needed or to thank Him for something that has been received. As any loving earthly father would be, God is interested in all that happens to you.

And He is looking forward to spending some time alone with you tomorrow and every day!

The Secret

I met with God in the morning
When the day was at its best,
And His presence came like sunrise
Like a glory within my breast.

All day long the presence lingered
All day long He stayed with me;
And we sailed in perfect calmness
O'er a very troubled sea.

Other ships were blown and battered,
Other ships were sore distressed;
But the winds that seemed to drive them
Brought to us a peace and rest.

Then I thought of other mornings,
With a keen remorse of mind,
When I too, had loosed the moorings,
With His presence left behind.

So I think I know the secret
Learned from many a troubled way;
You must seek God in the morning
If you want Him through the day.

— Ralph S. Cushman
Spiritual Hilltops

---

[1] "The Father looks for men who will worship Him..." (John 4:23 *Phillips*)

[2] "For now we are all children of God through faith in Jesus Christ." (Gal. 3:26 *Living Bible*)

[3] "He is like a father to us, tender and sympathetic to those who reverence Him." (Psalm 103:13 *Living Bible*)

[4] "He is always thinking about you and watching everything that concerns you." (1 Peter 5:7 *Living Bible*)

[5] "In the morning, rising up a great while before day, He went out and departed into a solitary place, and there prayed." (Mark 1:35)

6 "Open my eyes to see wonderful things in your Word." (Psalm 119:18 *Living Bible*)

7 "Man shall not live by bread alone, but by every word that proceedeth out of the mouth of God." (Matt. 4:4)

8 "These are written, that ye might believe that Jesus is the Christ, the Son of God; and that believing ye might have life through His name." (John 20:31)

9 "Fix your thoughts on what is true and good and right. Think about things that are pure and lovely, and dwell on the fine, good things in others. Think about all you can praise God for and be glad about." (Phil. 4:8 *Living Bible*)

10 "I have thought much about your words, and stored them in my heart so that they would hold me back from sin." (Psalm 119:11 *Living Bible*)

11 "Praise Him for His mighty works. Praise His unequalled greatness... You praise Him! (Psalm 150:2-6 *Living Bible*)

12 "Don't forget to thank Him." (Phil. 4:6 *Living Bible*)

13 "If we freely admit that we have sinned, we find God utterly reliable and straightforward — He forgives our sins and makes us thoroughly clean from all that is evil." (1 John 1:9 *Phillips*)

14 "Don't just think about your own affairs, but be interested in others, too, and in what they are doing." (Phil. 2:4 *Living Bible*)

15 "Don't worry about anything; instead, pray about everything; tell God your needs..." (Phil. 4:6 *Living Bible*)

16 "If you want to know what God wants you to do, ask Him, and He will gladly tell you, for He is always ready to give a bountiful supply of wisdom to all who ask Him." (James 1:5 *Living Bible*)

17 "God is mighty, and yet He regards nothing as trivial. He is mighty in power of understanding." (Job 36:5 *Berkeley Version*)

18 "We have such confidence in Him that we are certain that he hears every request that is made in accord with His own plan. And since we know that He invariably gives His attention to our prayers, whatever they are about, we can be quite sure that our prayers will be answered." (1 John 5:14-15 *Phillips*)

 PPENDIX B

Scripture Memory

Scripture Memory is taking God's Word and hiding it in our heart for guidance, protection, and encouragement. We will not always have our Bibles with us, but we can never be separated from the verses we have memorized.

Why Memorize Scripture?

Why should Christians memorize Scripture?

☑ First and foremost, we are *commanded* to learn God's Word and meditate upon it (Deut. 6:6-7; Josh. 1:8; Col. 3:16).

☑ Another reason is that memorizing Scripture *helps keep us from sin* (Psalm 37:31; 119:9-11; Matt. 4:1-10).

☑ It *transforms our minds to think God's thoughts* (Rom. 12:1–2), *enables the Holy Spirit to guide us* (Prov. 6:20-22), and *gives us a working knowledge of the Bible* (Psalm 119:105).

☑ Scripture memory also helps equip us for *witnessing* (I Peter 3:15; Acts 18:28) and *counseling those in need* (I Thess. 2:13).

☑ Hiding God's Word in our hearts helps *produce spiritual growth* in our lives (I Peter 2:2; Acts 20:32).

How to Memorize Scripture

The first step in beginning a program of Scripture memory is to *realize its importance*. Memorizing takes disciplined effort — W-O-R-K. We must understand the benefits of Scripture Memory if we are to continue to exert our minds in learning new verses.

A second step is to *set a realistic goal*. Within this self-study course, we have suggested 2 verses per week. This will allow you plenty of time during the week not only for new memory work, but also to review previous verses you have learned. Studies have shown if you review a new verse every day for two months, and then once per month after that, you will remember it when you need it.

A third step is to *formulate a plan*. Decide what you will memorize, and when and where. If you fail to plan your memory work, you are planning to fail! You can follow one of the many helpful memory plans devised by different organizations or pick meaningful verses and/or passages to help you in your personal life and ministry. You may choose to write out your verses on a sheet of paper, a 3' x 5' card, or the small verse cards specially designed for Scripture Memory (available in Christian bookstores).

When you actually memorize, the following tips will help you be more effective:

1. Read the context around the verse to see what the verse is really teaching.

2. Work on one phrase at a time.

3. Memorize out loud, if possible.

4. Memorize word perfect.

5. Repeat the verse with the reference "before" and "after." This will help you remember not only the verse but also where it is found.

6. Meditate on what the verse is saying.
    a) Visualize it.
    b) Share it.
    c) Sing it.
    d) Pray it.
    e) Apply it (Ezra 7:10)

Finally, *count on God's help as you memorize*. He wants you to learn his Word and will give you the wisdom and strength to do so!

When are Good Times to Memorize and Review Verses?

A common excuse for not memorizing Scripture is "I just don't have time." While the truth of that statement can be debated (we *make* time for the things that are important to us), what people need to realize is that there are many times when you can "kill two birds with one stone" and memorize Scripture while involved in other activities. For example, you can learn verses while *waiting for an appointment* or *riding in a car* (while driving it is best to concentrate on the road!). Many people memorize when they *walk* or *exercise*. Others memorize while performing routine daily tasks: *brushing their teeth, shaving, washing the dishes*. The possibilities are endless if you will only look around!

A Practical Review System

Someone has stated that there are three secrets to Scripture Memory:

1) Review

2) Review

3) Review

Even if we learn a verse perfectly, it will not stay with us unless we review periodically.

When you are working on a new verse, you should review it several times daily. This will help you learn it quickly. Review each recently memorized verse every day for two months. This firmly plants the verse in your mind. Finally, reviewing all your verses at least once a month will help keep them fresh in your mind — ready to use!

KNOWING GOD

PART I

A three-part series, to
help you understand how *you* can know
God personally, follow His ways,
and share Him with others.

GOD'S PURPOSE:
PEACE AND LIFE

God loves you and wants you to experience peace and eternal life.

The Bible says...

"...we have peace with God through our Lord Jesus Christ." Romans 5:1

"For God loved the world so much that he gave his only Son, so that everyone who believes in him may not die but have eternal life." John 3:16

Since God planned for us to have peace and the full life right now, why are most people not having it?

OUR PROBLEM:
SEPARATION

God created us to be like Him and enjoy life. He did not force us to love and obey Him, but gave us a will and freedom of choice.

The first man and woman chose to disobey God and go their own willful way. We still make this choice today. This results in separation from God.

The Bible says...

"Everyone has sinned and is far away from God's saving presence." Romans 3:23

"For sin pays its wage—death; but God's free gift is eternal life in union with Christ Jesus our Lord." Romans 6:23

Through the ages, individuals have tried in many ways to cross this gap...without success...

MAN
Unholy
-lying
-stealing

Our decision results in separation from God.

GOD
Holy

GOD'S ANSWER: JESUS CHRIST

Jesus Christ is the only answer to this problem. He died on the Cross and rose from the grave, took the punishment for our sin and bridged the gap between God and man.

The Bible says...

"For there is one God, and there is one who brings God and mankind together, the man Christ Jesus." 1 Timothy 2:5

"But God has shown us how much he loves us—it was while we were still sinners that Christ died for us!" Romans 5:8

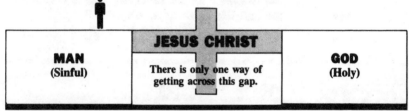

OUR RESPONSE: RECEIVE CHRIST

We must trust Jesus Christ and receive Him by personal surrender and invitation.

The Bible says (Christ is Speaking)...

"Listen! I stand at the door and knock; if anyone hears my voice and opens the door, I will come into his house and eat with him, and he will eat with me." Revelation 3:20

"Some, however, did receive him and believed in him; so he gave them the right to become God's children." John 1:12

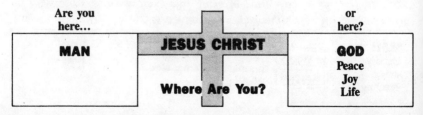

BEGINNING WITH CHRIST

Is there any good reason why you do not want to invite Jesus Christ into your life right now?

How to begin your life with Christ:

1. Admit your condition (I am a sinner).
2. Be willing to turn from your sins (repent).
3. Believe that Jesus Christ died for you on the Cross and rose from the grave.
4. Through prayer, invite Jesus Christ to come in and control your life through the Holy Spirit. (Receive Him as Lord and Savior.)

CONFESSING CHRIST

The Bible Says...

"If you confess that Jesus is Lord and believe that God raised him from death, you will be saved." Romans 10:9

EXAMPLE OF WHAT TO PRAY
(Make it your prayer):

Dear Lord Jesus,

I know that I am a sinner and need Your forgiveness. I believe that You died for my sins. I want to turn from my sins. I now invite You to come in my life. I trust You as Savior and follow You as Lord.

Thank you, Lord, for saving me. Amen.

Date	Signature

GOD'S ASSURANCE: HIS WORD

If you prayed this prayer,

The Bible says...

"Everyone who calls out to the Lord for help will be saved." Romans 10:13

"For it is by God's grace that you have been saved through faith. It is not the result of your own efforts, but God's gift, so that no one can boast about it." Ephesians 2:8,9

Did you sincerely ask Jesus Christ to come into your life? Where is He right now? What has He given you?

The Bible says...

"Whoever has the Son has this life; whoever does not have the Son of God does not have life. I am writing this to you so that you may **know** that you have eternal life—you that believe in the Son of God." 1 John 5:12,13

WALKING WITH GOD

This is the **beginning of** a wonderful **new life** in Christ. To deepen this walk with Christ:

1. Read your Bible every day to get to know Christ better.

2. Talk to God in prayer every day.

3. Be controlled by the Holy Spirit.

4. Tell others about Christ.

5. Share your new life by your love and concern for others.

6. Find another Christian or two with whom you can pray and share regularly your successes and failures.

7. Worship and serve with other Christians in a church where Christ is preached.

God bless you as you do.

*To help you walk
with God, read
FOLLOWING CHRIST*

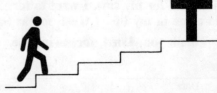

FOLLOWING CHRIST
PART II

STUDY THE BIBLE

Now that you are a Christian, the best way to "continue to grow in the grace and knowledge of our Lord and Savior Jesus Christ" (2 Peter 3:18) is to start studying the Bible right away.
Use your Bible to study the verses
listed in this booklet.

The Bible says. . .

"All Scripture is inspired by God and is useful for teaching the truth, rebuking error, correcting faults, and giving instruction for right living, so that the person who serves God may be fully qualified and equipped to do every kind of good deed" (2 Timothy 3:16, 17).

Steps for Growth through Bible Study

Beginning with one chapter of the Gospel of Luke each day, ask yourself these questions:

1. What does it say and mean?
2. What does this teach me about God?
3. What does this teach me about how to live daily?
    a. what good things to do
    b. what bad things to avoid
4. What commands or promises do I find here to obey or receive?

PRAY DAILY

Prayer is talking to God. It may seem strange at first, but as you continue, prayer will become more meaningful. Start each day with prayer, and pray throughout the day. Take all your problems to God. He is interested in everything you do (1 Peter 5:7).

Daily through prayer:

1. Thank and praise God (Philippians 4:4-7)
2. Ask for and receive His wisdom (James 1:5)
3. Seek His forgiveness when you sin (1 John 1:8-10)
4. Take your problems to God and claim His promises (1 Peter 5:7)

Suggestions for Daily Times with God

1. Plan a daily time with God (Mark 1:35).
2. Find a quiet place (Psalm 46:10).
3. Record requests and keep track of God's answers.
4. Read a chapter in Luke; then pray about your plans for the day.
5. Remind yourself all day long that God is with you.

DEPEND ON THE HOLY SPIRIT

The Holy Spirit lives in every believer and His work is to:

1. Teach us more about God (John 14:26)
2. Guide us moment by moment (Romans 8:14)
3. Assure us that we are truly God's children (Romans 8:16, 17)
4. Pray for us (Romans 8:26)
5. Help us walk victoriously (Galatians 5:16)
6. Fill us with God's love (Romans 5:5)
7. Make us more like Jesus (2 Corinthians 3:18)
8. Help us tell others about Jesus (Acts 1:8)

Meditate on John 1:32

Read, study, and meditate on the above Scriptures. Allow the Holy Spirit, through these truths, to control your life daily.

WORSHIP REGULARLY

When you received Jesus Christ you became a member of the "Body of Christ."

The Bible says. . .

"They spent their time in learning from the apostles, taking part in the fellowship, and sharing in the fellowship meals and the prayers" (Acts 2:42).

God's Word instructs all believers to worship regularly. You are to:

1. Love, correct and strengthen one another (Hebrews 10:24, 25)
2. Be taught, equipped for service, and rooted in the faith (Ephesians 4:11-16)
3. Learn to serve others (Romans 12:4-21)
4. Worship the Lord by:
   a. Praising Him (Psalm 149:1)
   b. Telling publicly about the good things He has done for you (Psalm 107:8)

You should support the church with your prayers, tithes, and abilities.

SERVE OTHERS

We have been saved to serve (Ephesians 2:8-10). The Bible is filled with examples of those who served. Christ was a servant (Philippians 2:5-8). He washed His disciples' feet and commanded us to serve others in similar ways (John 13:14).

You won't have to look far to find someone in need. Serve Christ, the church, and those in need in your community.

1. Live out your faith by serving (Ephesians 2:8-10).
2. Help others by serving (Luke 22:27).
3. Bear one another's burdens by serving (Galatians 6:2).
4. Witness by serving (1 Corinthians 9:19-23).
5. Lead by serving (Mark 10:43-45).

CONQUER YOUR DOUBTS, FEARS

At times, you may doubt that you are God's child. Satan will point to failures, problems, or unconfessed sin in your life. When that happens, you must remember that you are not saved by your own goodness, but by what Christ did for you on the Cross. Remember that you are:

1. Redeemed and forgiven (Ephesians 1:7)
2. Safe in His hands (John 10:27-29)
3. Secure in His love (Romans 8:35-39)
4. Kept by His power (1 Peter 1:3-5)

Meditate on the above passages. Do not rely on your feelings. Believe God's Word.

Remember... God said it in His Word.
I believe it in my heart.
That settles it in my mind.

LIVE ONE DAY AT A TIME

Too often our lives are filled with worry about possible future problems. Most of the things we worry about never happen. Live one day at a time, believing that God's grace will be sufficient to meet each day's demands (2 Corinthians 12:9).

The Bible says. . .

"So do not worry about tomorrow: it will have enough worries of its own. There is no need to add to the troubles each day brings" (Matthew 6:34).

Let God help you through each day. He is able. Remember:
1. Don't worry about anything, but pray about everything (Philippians 4:6-7)
2. Cast all your cares upon God (1 Peter 5:7)
3. Forget the past and walk on (Philippians 3:13)
4. God will never leave you nor forsake you (Hebrews 13:5)
5. God will supply all your needs through Christ (Philippians 4:19)

FIND BLESSING IN TESTING

Things like sickness, money problems, and other difficulties will happen even though you have Christ in your life.

But the Bible says that God has a reason for allowing such times of testing:

1. Testing has good results (Romans 8:28,29)
2. Testing develops character (James 1:2-4)
3. Testing builds hope (James 5:3, 4)
4. Testing makes Christ real (2 Corinthians 4:8-17)
5. Testing matures the Christian (1 Peter 5:8-10)

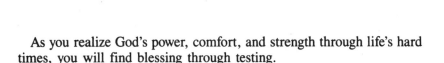

As you realize God's power, comfort, and strength through life's hard times, you will find blessing through testing.

MEETING TEMPTATION

Temptation is a natural part of every believer's life (1 Corinthians 10:13). Jesus met temptation through the help of the Holy Spirit by using Bible passages. So can you (Luke 4:1-14).

The following guidelines will help you overcome temptation:
1. Pray (Matthew 26:41)

2. Put on God's armor (Ephesians 6:10-18)

3. Learn to walk in the Spirit (Galatians 5:16, 17)

4. Run from youthful lusts (2 Timothy 2:22)

5. Resist the devil (James 4:7)

God will help you overcome temptation if you trust Him.

TELLING OTHERS ABOUT CHRIST

Sharing your new life in Christ with others, by word and actions, is one of the most satisfying and exciting experiences you will ever have. The more you express your faith, the stronger it will become and the easier it will be to share.

Here are some Scriptures to help you tell others about Christ (Matthew 4:19).

1. Let your life witness for Christ (Matthew 5:16).
2. Prepare and be ready for times to share Christ (1 Peter 3:15).
3. Trust the Holy Spirit for boldness (Acts 1:8).
4. Pray that God will use you.

*See the next booklet,
SHARING CHRIST
for more instruction
on witnessing.*

HELP IN TIME OF NEED

When facing temptation...........................James 1:2-4 & 12-15
1 Corinthians 10:13

When seeking guidance.............................Proverbs 3:5, 6
James 1:5

When needing forgiveness............................1 John 1:9
Hebrews 4:15, 16

When burdened with many problems....................Psalm 55:22
1 Peter 5:7

When facing danger ....Psalm 91
Psalm 121

When in financial need..............................Psalm 34:10
Philippians 4:19

When your patience is tried.........................James 1:2-4
Romans 8:28, 29

When doubting your salvation.........................1 John 5:11-13
John 3:16

SHARING CHRIST
PART III

INTRODUCTION

The more you realize what Christ has done for you, the more you will want to share with others the Good News about Him.

As Christians, we are friends for Christ (2 Corinthians 5:17-20). We are to help bring those separated from God by sin back to God through faith in Christ. We do this by pointng them to Jesus.

THE HAND OF GOD IN SHARING

There is more to sharing Christ than using a few Scripture verses. Scripture is very important, but involved also are **our life, the Holy Spirit, and the Hand of God.**

**A friend
for Christ
Acts 8:26-35**

Read the story and learn how God worked out all the details.
Expect God to help you tell someone about Jesus today!

SHARING BY LIFE

Your life is a great part of your witness. Philip, one of the early witnesses, was known for his Christian character (Acts 6:3). You are like a letter from Christ, and are "known and read" by others (2 Corinthians 3:2, 3).

Someone has said, "What you **are** speaks so loudly, I cannot hear what you **say**." How does your life read to others? Has Christ made changes in your life?

When we live for Jesus, others who know us will want to know Him too. Your life will shine for Him (Matthew 5:13-16).

SHARING THE WORD (GOSPEL)

The "Gospel" is the good news that Jesus died for sinners, was buried, and rose again (1 Corinthians 15:1-4). It is "the power to save all who believe" (Romans 1:16). Knowing and sharing Scripture is very important in effective witnessing.

1. God's Word is a **seed** through which we are born again
   (1 Peter 1:23).
2. God blesses the planting of His Word (Isaiah 55:11).
3. We can all plant "good seed." Paul said, "I have planted, Apollos watered; but God gave the increase"
   (1 Corinthians 3:6, 7).

Learn the verses in KNOWING GOD, and master the use of the illustrations.

Pray for opportunities to share the Gospel with other people. Team up with other Christians for mutual encouragement.

SHARING WITH POWER

You aren't alone when sharing the Gospel. "For the Spirit that God has given us does not make us timid; instead his Spirit fills us with power" (2 Timothy 1:7).

The Holy Spirit will:

1. Teach us God's Word and refresh our memories (John 14:26)
2. Help us speak with authority (Matthew 10:19, 20)
3. Give power for our witness (Acts 1:8)

God's Word is the "Sword of the Spirit" (Ephesians 6:17). We must be sure our lives are clean, our hearts are right with God, and we are fully yielded to the Holy Spirit. When Stephen spoke, "the Spirit gave Stephen such wisdom that when he spoke, they could not refute him" (Acts 6:5-10).

Pray daily to be filled and empowered by the Holy Spirit.

PLANS FOR SHARING

To plant the seed, there has to be soil. The Gospel needs a human heart, but where do we find prepared hearts? A proven plan, called "Operation Andrew," might help you start. Andrew met Jesus and brought his brother to Jesus.

Here's the plan:

1. List several people you know who are not Christians: friends, neighbors, or people at work or school.

Name _____

Name _____

2. Pray regularly that God will open doors for you to witness to them.
3. Do things for and with these people to show you care. Build friendship by showing Christ's love over a period of time.
4. Invite them to a Christian film showing, a Bible study, or any special event where the Gospel is explained.

5. Attempt to bring them to a place of commitment. They may be ready after hearing the Gospel for the first time, or it might take several sharing experiences.

Ask questions such as:

• What did you think of the meeting, speaker, film, or Bible study?

• Have you ever received Jesus Christ as your personal Savior, or are you thinking about it?

• What do you believe about life after death?

• Where do you think you will spend eternity?

• If you were to die today, would you go to heaven? Why should God accept you in His heaven?

Ask any of these questions to find out what they believe. Are they trusting in Christ? If not, would they like to? If they are open, share KNOWING GOD.

SHARING "KNOWING GOD"

KNOWING GOD is a booklet which you can easily read with another in five minutes. It contains everything that a person needs to know to become a Christian . . . when the Holy Spirit is at work in the person's life.

It can be given as a Gospel tract. You can leave it with people to read, and get their response later. The best use is to **read through it with an individual,** giving proper emphasis where necessary and sharing additional Scriptures and illustrations.

The Facts

While holding the booklet so that the person with whom you are talking can see it, read it slowly. **As you read, circle key words and underline key phrases.** Look carefully at the pictures and make comments. Share the entire booklet.

The Invitation

After sharing the facts—the Good News—ask, "Which side of the Cross are you on? Have you received Christ as your personal Savior? (Romans 10:9) Is there any good reason why you cannot do so right now?"

If they are willing, turn to the prayer of commitment.

Prayer of Commitment

Lead them out loud, phrase by phrase, through the prayer. Romans 10:13 tells us that "everyone who calls out to the Lord for help will be saved." Let them call on the name of the Lord.

Review with them:

- Christ came in (Revelation 3:20)

- I'm a child of God (John 1:12)

- I am saved from my sins (Romans 10:9)

God's Assurance

Read through the assurance page, emphasizing the fact that we can **know**. The Bible says so. Then make sure they read FOLLOWING CHRIST.

FOLLOW-UP

Be faithful to follow up a new Christian like a good spiritual parent. You cannot take the place of the pastor or church, but you can help the person get started right. Offer spiritual feeding, protection from the evil one, and training to anyone you lead to Christ.

Do the following:

- Continue to pray for them.
- Share the booklet FOLLOWING CHRIST.
- Be sure they attend a church where the Bible is taught.
- Help them get involved in a Bible study group.
- Keep in touch for encouragement.
- Encourage them to pray and share Christ with others.

ᴀᵖᵖᵉⁿᵈⁱˣ APPENDIX D

THE BRIDGE ILLUSTRATION

One of the advantages of this presentation is that it is effective cross-culturally and can be drawn on a piece of paper, then left in the inquirer's possession to review what may have transpired. On a sample piece of paper draw two horizontal lines about two inches apart, then

Begin by writing GOD on the right line and PEOPLE on the left line. State that in the beginning God made each person to have fellowship with him, but each person chose to go his or her own way, turned his or her back on God, rebelled against him, and so fell into sin. This caused a separation between people and God (draw the two sides of the cliff on God's side and people's side).

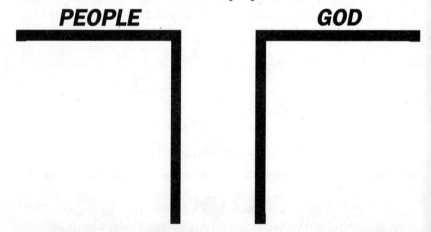

PEOPLE   **GOD**

We know that a great separation exists between God and individuals because the Bible tells us that "all have sinned and come short of the glory of God" (Romans 3:23). Write the word SIN vertically between the two sides of the cliff, and write Romans 3:23 under the side of People, noting under it, "All have sinned," then circle the word "all." Now quote Romans 6:23, write it down under the People side, and note under it, "Sin earns spiritual death." Then quote Hebrews 9:27, write it down, and put down, "Judgment is coming." Then say, "This is the BAD NEWS, and write it down at the bottom. At this point a person is in a hopeless and helpless condition with no way of crossing the chasm.

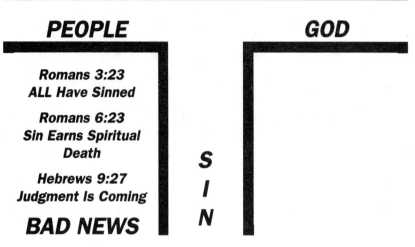

Then quote Romans 5:8, and, as you are quoting it, draw the cross over the term "sin" by drawing the lines starting from God's side. Write down Romans 5:8 and "Christ died for us" underneath the side of God. Now quote Ephesians 2:8-9, write it down, and note, "Redemption is a free gift." (God's grace is absolutely free.) Then quote John 1:12, and as you are quoting it write "Believe" on the left side of the cross and "Receive" on the right; write the reference down on God's side with this notation under it: "We must believe and receive Jesus as Lord and Savior." Then say, "This is the GOOD NEWS, and write it on the bottom of that side. This now is the *only* way a person can cross the chasm of sin that separates the individual from God.

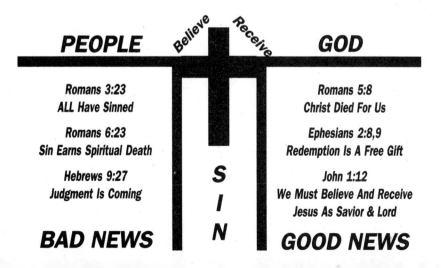

The sinner then believes (puts his or her total trust in) that Jesus' death on the cross paid the penalty for the individual's sin, then receives Christ into his or her life through a prayer that invites him to come in and take over. The result of this "transaction" is that Scripture now gives us assurance that a person then becomes a child of God. When a person confesses Christ as Lord and Savior and believes in his atoning work on his or her behalf, the person is saved — quote Romans 10:9-10, and write it over the whole illustration.

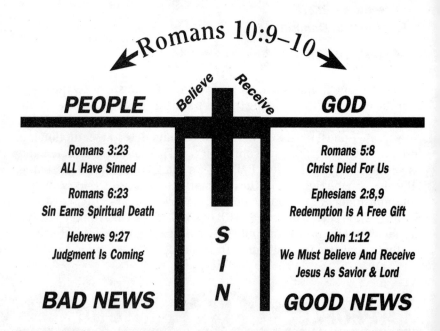

$\mathcal{A}$PPENDIX E

Dawson Trotman Transcriptions

Session 1

"God didn't make just a whole mass of people and shoot them on down. He made two. And the first order He ever gave man and woman was be fruitful and not add but multiply. And the rule He made for vegetables and fruit and birds and bees and fish and human beings was that each by a union or a pollination or germination should reproduce after their kind and that everything that was produced—now get it, this is the point—that everything that was produced would not only be like the parents but would have its seed in itself to reproduce. The first chapter of Genesis gives us the clue— 'Whose seed is in itself... whose seed is in itself.' The cows, 'Whose seed is in itself.' You know, when the Lord sent the flood and destroyed all flesh of man because he was so wicked and of course along with it went a lot of the animals and the Lord had the ark, this great massive ship four hundred feet long loaded to the gills with all kinds of different things. And they put two—a male and a female of every species. In some cases they put seven. I presume those were more like cattle and all. And you know, I often get a kick talking to people— 'When I see old Noah, I'm gonna say Noah old boy—put her there. I just want to thank you old fella. That was a big tough job building that ship and getting all those bulls and cows on there. But you know, very often when I'm eating a Filet Mignon or a nice big old piece of cheese or ice cream or drinking a cool glass of milk, I used to think 'Good old Noah!'. Boy, if he hadn't... They didn't need very much but you know what—every one of those beasts had to have the seed in itself. They had a job to do. Everything else was subsidiary. Everything else was secondary. The very first thing that God... God didn't tell Adam and Eve to be spiritual. They were created spiritual. They were in His image. They were like God. He just said, 'Now I want more of you. Be fruitful and multiply.' And listen gang, the secret of the spread of the Gospel to the four ends of the earth around the world, down into every little nook and cranny of every little town and hamlet is this plan. But we've been robbed of it. Somehow along the line we lost something in our Christianity."

"Are you producing? If not, why not? Is it lack of communion with Christ your Lord? That closeness of fellowship which is part of the great plan. Or is it some sin in the life—unconfessed—something that has stopped the flow? Or is it are you still a babe? 'When for the time you ought to be teachers, you have need that one teach you again.' The problem of the fact that we are not getting this Gospel to the ends of the earth isn't because it isn't potent enough. I'm not going to tell the story, but only refer to a fact or two. 23 years ago, we took a sailor. And we spent some time with him and showed him how to reproduce after his kind. It took time. It wasn't a little hurried 30 minute challenge in a church service and a hurried 'good-bye and come back next week'. But we spent time together. And we took care of his problems, and taught him how not only to hear God's Word and to read God's Word but how to study God's Word. And not only how to study it but how to fill the quiver of his heart with the arrows of God's Word that the Spirit of God could lift an arrow from that quiver and place it to the bow of his lips and pierce a heart for it. And he found a number of boys on the ship, but none of them would go all out. They'd go to church, but when it came right down to doing something... And he came to me after a month of this and he said, 'Daws,' he says, 'I can't get any of these guys on the ship down to business.' And I said, 'Listen, you ask God to give you one. You can't have two until you have one. Ask for one. Ask God to give you a man after your own heart.' He began to pray. One day he came and said, 'I think I found him'. Later he brought him over—it was three months from the time I started to work with him. And he found a man. A man of like-heart. He wasn't the kind of a guy you had to push and give prizes to do something for God. He loved the Lord and he was willing to pay a price to produce. And he worked with him. And those two fellas began to grow and they each produced in their own lives. And on that ship, 125 men found the Savior before it was sunk at Pearl Harbor. And men off of that first battle ship through this particular line are in four continents of the world as missionaries today. And it spread to another ship and another ship, and when the Japanese struck at Pearl Harbor there was a work going forward on 50 ships of the

US. fleet. And when the war closed there was a work—one or more producers—I'm not talking about Christians—I'm talking about producers. One or more men who were not sterile—fathers. One or more on a thousand ships of the US. fleet, and that many army camps and air bases. Because it had a start. It had to have a start and the devil's great trick is to stop it. And if he can stop it in you now, he's done the big job."

Session Eight

"When Ruthie was three and Bruce was five — when Bruce was three he could quote 18 verses correctly with the references for and aft. He started on his third birthday learning three a week for six weeks. I just did that to prove to some of these grown-ups it could be done, you see. Well, they'd go up to Grandpa and Grandma's and Grandpa would put little Ruthie there and little Bruce there and he'd say, 'Now, Mary had a little lamb,' and they'd look at him kinda funny. Or he'd say, 'Little boy blue' and they'd look at him — 'Well, who's little boy blue?' And he thought they were kinda dumb, so the mother said, 'They know some things. Give them Romans 3:23, Bruce.' Ahhh! And he quoted Romans 3:23. And he said, 'Shall I quote another one Grandpa?' 'Sure.' And he started quoting and he quoted five, ten, fifteen — and Ruth would quote some in between. And boy, he thought, 'I am the Grandpa!' And he took them over to the neighbors and over to the Aunts and over to the Uncles and showed them how great these young kids were, but the Word of God was doing its work. And it wasn't very many weeks until the Holy Spirit through the voices of babes planted the seed in their hearts. 'Out of the mouths of babes and sucklings hast Thou ordained strength.' Soul winners are not soul winners because of what they know. It's because of whom they know and how well they know Him and how much they long for others to know Him — those are your soul winners. Oh, but I am afraid! 'The fear of man bringeth a snare, but who so puteth his trust in the Lord shall be safe.' There is no reason under God's heaven but sin and immaturity and lack of communion that will put you in a position where you can't produce. And there isn't anything under God's heaven that's gonna keep that new born-again one from growing on with the Lord if he has a mammy or a pappy or someone to take care of him and to give him that which God has provided for the new babe for his normal, natural growth. The effects of them thereby causes irresistible laws and you sow the seed and you'll get results. Not in every heart and not every time the seed is sown is there a soul born. But there'll be a soul born, these others things being right. And when it's born, you give it the care that Paul gave. Paul believed in it. He was a great evangelist, but he had time for follow-up. The New Testament is largely made up of the letters of Paul which were the follow-up letters to the converts. James believed in it— 'Be doers of the Word and not hearers only.' Peter believed in it— 'As new born babes desire the sincere milk of the Word.' John believed in it—he said, 'I have no greater joy than to hear that my children walk in the faith.' And all the writings of Peter and Paul and James and most of the writings of John—first, second and third John—are food for the new Christian. The Gospel spread to the then-known world in the first century without radio, television, printing press and all because each produced one was a reproducer. But no, today we've got a lot of pew sitters. We've got a lot of people who think that if they're faithful in church and put good size gifts in the collection plate and get other people to come, they've done their deeds. Where's your man—where's your woman—where's your boy, where's your girl? Every one of you. I don't care how old you are."

APPENDIX F

SELECTED BIBLIOGRAPHY

Disciplemaking

Adams, Jay E. *Godliness through Discipline*. Nutley, New Jersey: Presbyterian and Reformed Publishing Company, 1972.

Bertolucci, John. *The Disciplines of a Disciple*. Ann Arbor, Michigan: Servant Books, 1985.

Bonhoeffer, Dietrich. *The Cost of Discipleship*. London: SCM Press, 1959.

Bridges, Jerry. *The Practice of Godliness*. Colorado Springs, Colorado: NavPress, 1983.

_____. *The Pursuit of Holiness*. Colorado Springs, Colorado: NavPress, 1978.

Bruce, A. B. *The Training of the Twelve*. New York: Harper & Row, Publishers, n.d.

Chandapilla, P. T. *The Master Trainer*. Bombay: Gospel Literature Service, 1974.

Christian Life and Witness, The. Billy Graham Evangelistic Association,

Coleman, Robert E. *Growing in the Word*. Old Tappan, New Jersey: Fleming H. Revell Company, 1982.

_____. *The Master Plan of Discipleship*. Old Tappan, New Jersey: Fleming H. Revell Company, 1987.

_____. *The Master Plan of Evangelism*. Old Tappan, New Jersey: Fleming H. Revell Company, 1963.

_____. *The Mind of the Master*. Old Tappan, New Jersey: Fleming H. Revell Company, 1977.

Coppedge, Allan. *The Biblical Principles of Discipleship*. Grand Rapids, Michigan: Zondervan Publishing House, 1989.

Cosgrove, Francis M., Jr. *Essentials of Discipleship*. Colorado Springs, Colorado: NavPress, 1980.

_____. *Essentials of New Life*. Colorado Springs, Colorado: NavPress, 1978.

Dawson, David L. *"Equipping the Saints"* (A Four-volume syllabus). Available from the author, 5510 Lynn Street, Greenville, Texas 75401.

Discipleship Journal, The. Published by The Navigators, P. O. Box 6000, Colorado Springs, Colorado 80934 (bimonthly).

Edman, V. Raymond. *The Disciplines of Life*. Wheaton, Illinois: Scripture Press Publications, 1948.

Eims, LeRoy. *Disciples in Action*. Wheaton, Illinois: Victor Books, 1981.

_____. *The Lost Art of Disciple Making*. Grand Rapids, Michigan: Zondervan Publishing House, 1978.

_____. *No Magic Formula—Biblical Principles for Spiritual Warfare*. Colorado Springs, Colorado: NavPress, 1977.

_____. *What Every Christian Should Know About Growing*. Wheaton, Illinois: Victor Books, 1976.

Fish, Roy J. *Study Guide to The Master Plan of Evangelism*. Old Tappan, New Jersey: Fleming H. Revell Company, 1972.

Foster, Richard J. *Celebration of Discipline*, Revised Edition. San Francisco, California: Harper & Row, 1978, 1988.

Gardner, John E. *Personal Religious Discipline*. Grand Rapids, Michigan: William B. Eerdmans Publishing Company, 1966.

Getz, Gene A. *The Measure of a Church*. Glendale, California: Regal Books, 1975.

_____. *The Measure of a Family*. Glendale, California: Regal Books, 1976.

_____. *The Measure of a Man*. Glendale, California: Regal Books, 1974.

_____. *The Measure of a Woman*. Glendale, California: Regal Books, 1977.

Hadidian, Allen. *Discipleship—Helping Other Christians Grow*. Chicago: Moody Press, 1979, 1987.

Hanks, Billie, Jr. *If You Love Me*. Waco, Texas: Word Books, Publisher, 1985.

_____. *My Spiritual Notebook*. Waco, Texas: Word, Incorporated, 1977.

Henrichsen, Walter A. *Disciples Are Made—Not Born*. Wheaton, Illinois: Victor Books, 1974.

_____. *How to Disciple Your Children*. Wheaton, Illinois: Victor Books, 1981.

Holden, J. Stuart. *The Master and His Men*. London: Marshall, Morgan & Scott, 1953.

Horne, Herman Harrell. *Teaching Techniques of Jesus*. Grand Rapids, Michigan: Kregel Publications, 1964.

Hull, Bill. *Jesus Christ Disciplemaker*. Colorado Springs, Colorado: NavPress, 1984.

Hyde, Douglas. *Dedication and Leadership*. Notre Dame, Indiana: Notre Dame Press, 1966.

Kuhne, Gary W. *The Dynamics of Discipleship Training*. Grand Rapids, Michigan: Zondervan Publishing House, 1978.

_____. *The Dynamics of Personal Follow-up*. Grand Rapids, Michigan: Zondervan Publishing House, 1976.

McCasland, David C. *Open to Change*. Wheaton, Illinois: Victor Books, 1981. (A leader's guide is also available.)

MacDonald, Hope. *Discovering the Joy of Obedience*. Grand Rapids, Michigan: Zondervan Publishing House, 1980.

Mayhall, Jack. *Discipleship: The Price and the Prize*. Wheaton, Illinois: Victor Books, 1984.

Miller, Calvin. *The Taste of Joy, Recovering the Lost Glow of Discipleship*. Downers Grove, Illinois: InterVarsity Press, 1983.

Moore, Waylon B. *Multiplying Disciples—The New Testament Method for Church Growth*. Colorado Springs, Colorado: NavPress, 1981.

_____. *New Testament Follow-up*. Grand Rapids, Michigan: William B. Eerdmans Publishing Company, 1963.

NavLog. Quarterly information magazine published by The Navigators, P. O. Box 6000, Colorado Springs, Colorado 80934.

Pentecost, J. Dwight. *Design for Discipleship*. Grand Rapids, Michigan: Zondervan Publishing House, 1971.

Petersen, William J. *The Discipling of Timothy*. Wheaton, Illinois: Victor Books, 1980. (A leader's guide is also available.)

Phillips, Keith. *The Making of a Disciple*. Old Tappan, New Jersey: Fleming H. Revell Company, 1981.

Powell, Paul W. *The Complete Disciple*. Wheaton, Illinois: Victor Books, 1982. Riggs, Charles. *30 Discipleship Exercises*, An Equipping Tool. Minneapolis, Minnesota: Billy Graham Evangelistic Association, 1980.

Riggs, Charlie. *Learning to Walk with God*, Minneapolis, Mn: World Wide, 1986.

Robertson, Roy. *The Timothy Principle*. Colorado Springs, Colorado: NavPress, 1986.

Sanny, Lorne C. *Marks of a Disciple*. Colorado Springs, Colorado: NavPress, 1975.

Sargent, Rod. *Christians-in-the-Making*. Colorado Springs, Colorado: NavPress, 1981. (Booklet)

_____. *How to Handle Difficulties*. Colorado Springs, Colorado: NavPress, 1975. (Booklet)

Taylor, Richard Shelley. *The Disciplined Life*. Minneapolis, Minnesota: Bethany House Publishers, 1962.

Trotman, Dawson E. *Born to Reproduce*. Colorado Springs, Colorado: NavPress, 1975. (Booklet)

_____. *Coming to Christ Through Scripture Memory*. Colorado Springs, Colorado: NavPress, 1975. (Booklet)

_____. *Follow-up*. Colorado Springs, Colorado: NavPress, 1975. (Booklet)

_____. *The Need of the Hour*. Colorado Springs, Colorado: NavPress, 1975. (Booklet)

Verwer, George. *No Turning Back*. Wheaton, Illinois: Tyndale House Publishers, 1983.

Watson, David. *Called and Committed*. Wheaton, Illinois: Harold Shaw Publishers, 1982.

White, Jim. *Christlikeness*. Colorado Springs, Colorado: NavPress, 1976. (Booklet)

White, John. *The Race: Discipleship for the Long Run*. Downers Grove, Illinois: InterVarsity Press, 1984.

Wilson, Carl. *With Christ in the School of Disciple Building*. Grand Rapids, Michigan: Zondervan Publishing House, 1976.

Cassette tapes on a variety of discipleship-related subjects are available from The Discipleship Tape Library, 435 West Boyd, Norman, Oklahoma 73069, (405) 321-2810. Send for the current catalog and price list.

Video tapes for a number of the above books and discipleship concepts are available from International Evangelism Association, P. O. Box 6499, Fort Worth, Texas 76115, (817) 926-8465. Send for the current catalog and price list.

Evangelism

Aldrich, Joseph C. *Life-Style Evangelism*. Portland, Oregon: Multnomah Press, 1981.

Bleecker, Walter S. *The Non-Confronter's Guide to Leading a Person to Christ*. San Bernardino, California: Here's Life Publishers, 1990.

Bright, Bill. *Witnessing Without Fear*. San Bernardino, California: Here's Life Publishers, 1987.

Brooks, Hal. *Follow-up Evangelism*. Nashville, Tennessee: Broadman Press, 1972.

Chapman, John. *Know and Tell the Gospel*. Colorado Springs, Colorado: NavPress, 1985.

Coleman, Robert E. *The Heartbeat of Evangelism*. Colorado Springs, Colorado: NavPress, 1984. (Booklet)

Dawson, David L. *How to Share Your Testimony Effectively*. Singapore: Chin Long Printing Service, 1978.

Eims, LeRoy. *Winning Ways*. Wheaton, Illinois: Victor Books, 1974.

_____. *Laboring in the Harvest*. Colorado Springs, Colorado: NavPress, 1985.

Ford, Leighton. *Good News is for Sharing*. Elgin, Illinois: David C. Cook Publishing Co., 1977.

Heck, Joel. *The Art of Sharing Your Faith*. Tarrytown, New York: Fleming H. Revell Co., 1991.

Hendricks, Howard G. *Say It with Love*. Wheaton, Illinois: Victor Books, 1972. (A leader's guide is also available.)

Kennedy, D. James. *Evangelism Explosion*, Revised Edition. Wheaton, Illinois: Tyndale House Publishers, 1970, 1977.

Little, Paul E. *How to Give Away Your Faith*. Chicago: Inter-Varsity Press, 1966.

McCloskey, Mark. *Tell It Often—Tell It Well*. San Bernardino, California: Here's Life Publishers, 1985.

Metzger, Will. *Tell the Truth*. Downers Grove, Illinois: InterVarsity Press, 1981.

Peace, Richard. *Small Group Evangelism*, A Training Program for Reaching Out with the Gospel. Downers Grove, Illinois: InterVarsity Press, 1985.

Petersen, Jim. *Evangelism As a Lifestyle*. Colorado Springs, Colorado: NavPress, 1980.

_____. *Evangelism for Our Generation*. Colorado Springs, Colorado: NavPress, 1985.

Sanny, Lorne C. *The Art of Personal Witnessing*. Chicago: Moody Press, 1957.

Warren, Max. *I Believe in the Great Commission*. Grand Rapids, Michigan: William B. Eerdmans Publishing Company, 1976.

Watson, David. *I Believe in Evangelism*. Grand Rapids, Michigan: William B. Eerdmans Publishing Company, 1976.

Spiritual Gifts

Flynn, Leslie B. *19 Gifts of the Spirit*. Wheaton: Scripture Press, 1974.

Sanders, J. Oswald. *The Holy Spirit and His Gifts*. Zondervan, 1970.

Spiritual Gifts and Church Growth. Pasadena: Charles E. Fuller Institute of Evangelism and Church Growth, 1978.

Spiritual Gifts and Church Growth: Gifts Discovery Workshop. Pasadena: Charles E. Fuller Institute of Evangelism and Church Growth, 1982. Contains a helpful questionnaire to discern your own gift.

Yohn, Rick. *Discover Your Spiritual Gift and Use It*. Wheaton: Tyndale, 1974.